MODERN WORLD NATIONS

Ghana

Joseph R. Oppong
University of North Texas
and
Esther D. Oppong

Series Consulting Editor
Charles F. Gritzner
South Dakota State University

CHELSEA HOUSE
PUBLISHERS
A Haights Cross Communications Company

Philadelphia

Frontispiece: Flag of Ghana

Cover: Fishing boats with crab traps in Ghana.

CHELSEA HOUSE PUBLISHERS

VP, New Product Development Sally Cheney
Director of Production Kim Shinners
Creative Manager Takeshi Takahashi
Manufacturing Manager Diann Grasse

Staff for GHANA

Executive Editor Lee Marcott
Production Editor Jaimie Winkler
Picture Researcher 21st Century Publishing and Communications, Inc.
Cover Designer Keith Trego, Series Designer Takeshi Takahashi
Layout 21st Century Publishing and Communications, Inc.

A Haights Cross Communications Company

http://www.chelseahouse.com

First Printing

1 3 5 7 9 8 6 4 2

Library of Congress Cataloging-in-Publication Data

Oppong, Joseph R.
  Ghana / Joseph R. Oppong.
    p. cm.—(Modern world nations)
Includes index.
Contents: Introducing Ghana, the black star of Africa—Ghana's physical landscapes—
Ghana through time—Ghana's people and cultural diversity—Politics – Ghana style—
Making a living in Ghana—Life in Ghana today—What is the black star's future?
  ISBN 0-7910-7378-5
  1. Ghana—Juvenile literature. [1. Ghana.] I. Title. II. Series.
DT510 .O67 2002
966.7—dc21

                                                        2002015803

Table of Contents

Ghana

Located in the Kakum National Park and Conservancy, the famous canopy walk consists of seven hanging bridges. The bridges, held in place by ropes and wire, reach 80 feet (24 meters) above ground and offer remarkable viewing of the plants and animals living in the tropical rainforest canopy (tree crowns).

1

Introducing Ghana: The Black Star of Africa

Ghana was once called the "Gold Coast." This beautiful country located on West Africa's Guinea Coast, had so much gold that the first European visitors, the Portuguese, named it the Gold Coast. Its next-door neighbor, to the west, was called the Ivory Coast because of the abundance of ivory found there. Gold is found in several parts of West Africa, particularly the forest zone of modern Ghana. The West African gold trade was well established in ancient times. It linked the peoples of Ghana to the trans-Saharan commercial network that stretched from the West African forest zone across the Sahara to ports on the Mediterranean Sea.

European traders were drawn to the Gulf of Guinea by the lure of gold long before the slave trade began in this region. To the Europeans, Ghana was very important for these two reasons: gold and slaves. In fact, most of the slaves who were transported to the

United States were shipped from the Elmina Castle in Ghana.

Ghana is the geographic center of the world. The Greenwich (or prime) meridian, or 0 degrees longitude, passes through Ghana. The equator, 0 degrees latitude, passes through Ghana's territorial waters. So, when standing on the beautiful beaches of Ghana, one is standing literally at, or very close to, the geographic center of the world.

That is one reason why snow is never seen in Ghana. It never gets that cold. Ghana also lies right in the center of the West African coast, and shares borders with three French-speaking nations: Côte d'Ivoire (formerly Ivory Coast) to the west, Togo to the east, and Burkina Faso (formerly Upper Volta) to the north. The Gulf of Guinea and the Atlantic Ocean form Ghana's southern border. In fact, Ghana is an English-speaking island in a sea of French-speaking peoples.

Finally, Ghana was the first country in Africa south of the Sahara to become independent. In 1957, Ghana became the first African country to break away from colonial rule and to establish self-government of Africans by Africans. At the time of independence, Ghana enjoyed spectacular economic and political advantages that other countries in tropical Africa could only dream of having. The strong economy was based on timber, cocoa (the source of chocolate), of which Ghana was the world's leading producer, and gold.

Ghana had an excellent transportation network and the highest per capita income in Africa. Compared to other African countries, the educational system and the civil service were outstanding. With a parliamentary democracy, Ghana's future looked promising, and it seemed destined to be a leader in Africa.

Kwame Nkrumah, Ghana's first leader, saw the country as the "Star of Black Africa." Nkrumah's idea lives on with the black star that appears in the middle of Ghana's national flag. He believed that Ghana should lead the effort to free African countries from the shackles of colonialism. He also envisioned and worked hard for a union of independent African states. Nkrumah also helped found the Organization of African Unity and the Non-Aligned Movement, a grouping of countries that attempted to pursue policies independent of the Communist Eastern block and the capitalist West. Today, Nkrumah remains a hero throughout much of Africa, and his country, Ghana, is still known for spearheading African unity.

Unfortunately, Ghana also was the first African country to have a military takeover of its government. In 1966, a military coup removed Nkrumah from power. For the next quarter century, Ghana had almost a revolving door military rule that periodically was interspersed with brief civilian regimes. Instead of economic growth and prosperity, Ghanaians experienced huge declines in almost every sphere of life during this time. From the 1970s, life became so difficult that many Ghanaians left the country to seek better livelihoods elsewhere. Today, there are Ghanaians in almost every country in the world, including even Finland and the United States (Alaska included).

Amazingly, Ghana rebounded beginning in the late 1990s, and has re-emerged as a stable democracy and a leading player in African affairs. Partly in response to this, many Ghanaians who migrated during the 1970s and 1980s have been returning to live and work in Ghana. During this same period, many trained workers, particularly physicians and nurses, also left the country.

Ghana is not one of the biggest countries in Africa. At 92,090 square miles (238,513 square kilometers), it is slightly smaller than Oregon, or about the size of Illinois and Indiana combined. Ghana is also about the same size as the United Kingdom (UK), Ghana's leading trading partner and former colonial master. From its southernmost tip at Cape Three Points, which is only 4° 30' north of the equator to its northern-most point, 11° north latitude, Ghana extends about 420 miles (676 kilometers). The distance across the widest part, between longitude 1° 12' east and longitude 3° 15' west, measures about 350 miles (563 kilometers). Due to its location, Ghanaians

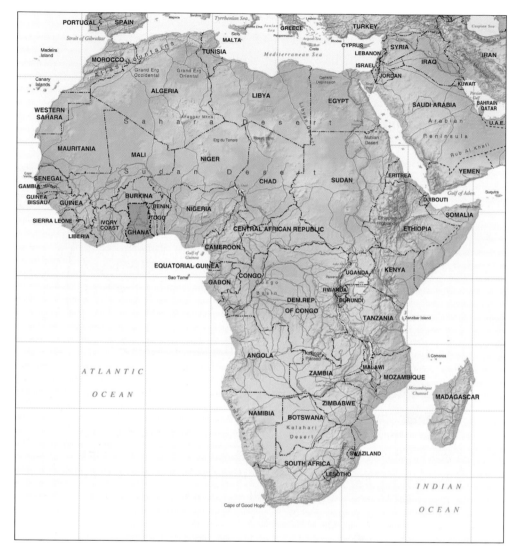

Ghana is located along the prime meridian (zero degrees longitude) and almost at the equator (zero degrees latitude), placing it nearly at the geographic center of the world. Ghana is the same size as Oregon or the United Kingdom and has about the same number of residents as New York State: 20 million people.

share the same time zone as the United Kingdom. The total population is slightly less than 20 million, about the same as New York State.

Ghana is a new country with an ancient name. The country

is named after the ancient empire of Ghana, from which ancestors of the country's present inhabitants are thought to have descended. Geographically, ancient Ghana was located 500 miles (805 kilometers) north of modern Ghana and occupied the area between the Senegal and Niger rivers. The modern nation of Ghana was formed from the merger of the Gold Coast (British colony) and the French Trust Territory of Togoland. On attaining independence in 1957, the country adopted the ancient name of Ghana. Having had a rough fight for freedom, Ghana proudly carries the motto of, "One people, one nation, one destiny."

An ancient past, an optimistic present, and a hopeful future all contribute to the exciting, beautiful, eternally green country of Ghana. In this book, the specific people, places, and things that make the country exclusively Ghanaian will be presented. The history of Ghana is an epic one, combining power struggle, tragedy, and victory. This book provides an exciting tour of a beautiful country that can boast of being full of gold, occupying the center of the world, and laying claim to a number of African "firsts." These pages convey Ghana's rich, golden history, and its fine and friendly people, including the current United Nations secretary-general, Kofi Annan. Readers will experience the lovely beaches and former slave castles, play soccer with the Ghana Black Stars, the national soccer team, and enjoy peanut butter soup. Welcome to Ghana, or as they say in Akan, one of Ghana's many languages, "*Akwaaba!*"

Ghana's 334-mile (538-kilometer) coastline on the Atlantic Ocean consists primarily of sandy shores. In western Ghana, the forest extends out directly to the beach. Moving inland, low-lying coastal plains dominate; over half of Ghana has an elevation of less than 500 feet (152 meters) above sea level.

Ghana's Physical Landscapes

The physical landscapes of Ghana offer a great variety of greenery with an assortment of tropical rain forests and park-like savannas. Even though the country is situated on the coast, there are still considerable changes in elevation. The coastline is mostly a sandy shore, behind which stretch the low-lying coastal plains. In the west, the forest reaches down to the sea. The forest belt, which extends northward from the western coast, is scattered in heavily forested hills. North of the forest, the rolling savanna is drained by the Black and White Volta Rivers, which join and flow southward to the sea.

The prairielike flatness of the land makes the smallest elevation look like a giant peak. The pleasant climate and the variety of plant and animal life will be explained. The natural environment plays a very important role in the everyday life of Ghanaians, and evidence of this will be seen in the following chapters. In fact, the economic activities in different parts of the country are carefully adapted to the natural environment and its varied conditions. Ghana provides an excellent illustration of what geographers call "cultural ecology," the close relationship between humans and the physical environment. Humans culturally adapt to, use, and modify the physical environments in which they live.

LAND FEATURES

Ghana is mainly a lowland. Half of the country lies at elevations lower than 500 feet (152 meters) above sea level. The highest point, Mount Afadjato, is only 2,905 (885 meters) feet tall. The coastline, which is 334 miles (538 kilometers) long, is mostly a low, sandy shore backed by plains and scrub and intersected by several rivers and streams. There are, however, no natural harbors in Ghana. All of the country's seaports are man-made. The coastline is smooth, not rugged. Most of the rivers are navigable only by canoe.

WEATHER AND CLIMATE

Imagine a country where it never snows, but where blue skies and bright sunshine are always abundant! Yet the cool sea breeze keeps daily temperatures along the coast at a comfortable 75°F (24°C). Temperatures of 100°F (38°C), which are common throughout much of the United States during summer months, do not occur in Ghana. These refreshing conditions describe the wonderful temperature of coastal Ghana. That is only part of the story, though. Residents also must contend with frequent, high humidity because of Ghana's proximity to the ocean. That is why summer temperatures of 70°F (21°C) can feel almost like 100°F (38°C). Climate is a very important factor to which people must adjust as they go about the daily tasks of living and working. Therefore, a closer look at Ghana's climate is worthwhile.

In order to understand atmospheric conditions, the

difference between weather and climate must be understood. Weather describes the atmosphere's condition at the moment. Climate, on the other hand, is the long-term average condition of the weather. Ghana's climate is tropical. Due to its location so close to the equator, the country receives an abundant supply of sunlight year-round. Except in a few places where high elevation lowers temperature, the annual temperature ranges between 79°F (26°C) and 84°F (29°C). Ghana has never experienced a temperature below 50°F (10°C), so there is not a clear winter season.

Climatic phenomena do not respect political boundaries. For example, winds, which carry moisture and influence temperature conditions circle freely around the earth. Thus, to understand the climate of a single country, knowing the general climate characteristics over a much broader area and especially the elements that influence local climate is essential. The major elements that influence Ghana's climate include prevailing air masses, latitudinal location, and continentality.

Two major air masses influence Ghana. They are the Tropical Continental Air Mass (cT), or the Northeast Tradewinds, and the Tropical Maritime Air Mass (mT), or Southwest Monsoons. The characteristics of an air mass depend mostly on its source region. The cT air mass, locally called the *harmattan*, originates over the Sahara desert, where temperatures are very high and relative humidity is very low. Consequently, these winds are hot and dry. In contrast, the Southwest Monsoon winds, which originate over the Atlantic Ocean, are cool and saturated with moisture. The zone where these two air masses meet is known as the Intertropical Convergence Zone (ITC). Most weather and climate experienced in West Africa is the result of these air masses and the location of the ITC.

Ghana has two main seasons: wet and dry. The seasons follow the apparent movement of the sun, seasonally northward and southward, back and forth across the equator. During the Northern Hemisphere summer, the warm and moist mT air mass intensifies and covers much of the country. The ITC moves north, bringing much of the southern part of the country under the influence of humid, maritime tropical air. This monsoon (seasonal winds) condition produces the heavy precipitation associated with the rainy season. As the sun returns south across the equator, the dry, dusty, tropical continental air mass originating over the Sahara Desert, the harmattan, prevails over much of the country. During this hot, dry season, many fires—both wild and of human origin—are common throughout much of the country, particularly in the north.

Generally in Ghana, as in other places, the more distant a location is from the ocean, the more extreme the temperature variations. Geographers call this continentality. This is due to the difference between heating of land and water. Land heats more quickly, but also loses heat more rapidly. In contrast, water heats much more slowly and loses heat more gradually. During the day, when the land is hot, the sea remains cooler. Winds blowing across the water bring relatively cool breezes to adjacent coastal areas. During the night, however, when the land loses its heat rapidly, the now warmer sea water warms the land. Thus, the lowest temperature range (difference between highest and lowest temperature) occurs near the coast. Highest ranges in temperature occur in the interior, far from the ocean.

In Ghana, due to continentality, the daily range of temperature is about 12°F to 13°F (-11°C to -10°C) at the coast, but as much as 18°F to 30°F (-8°C to -1°C) inland. Along the coast, both the lowest nighttime and monthly average temperature occurs in August. In the north, January is the coldest month. Over most of the country, the highest daily and monthly temperatures occur in February or March and the lowest occur in August.

Local conditions, particularly elevation, influence weather and climate throughout much of the country. Temperatures

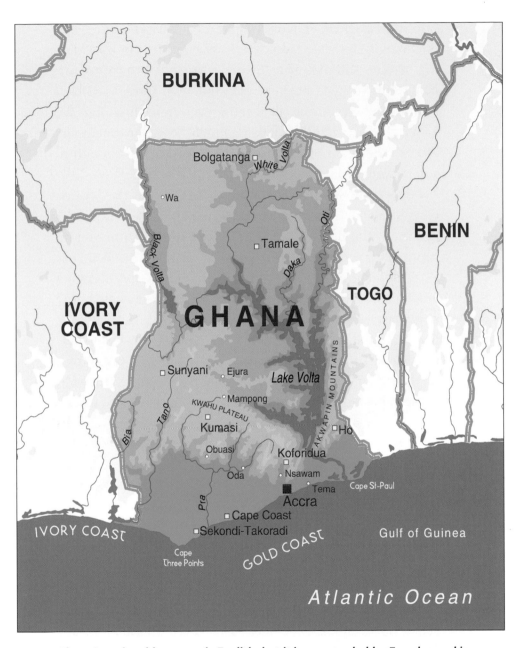

Ghana's national language is English, but it is surrounded by French-speaking countries. Ghana's smooth coastline has no natural harbors, and its rivers are navigable by canoes only. Due to its location along the coast, southern Ghana's temperatures are moderate, and there is high humidity and rainfall. Central and northern Ghana, which are influenced less by the ocean, are hotter and drier.

normally fall about 3°F (1.68°C) for each 1,000 feet (305 meters) of elevation above sea level. This is why eastern Africa's towering Mount Kilimanjaro, located very near the Equator, has a snow-capped peak. In the same way, places in Ghana with higher elevations, such as the Akwapim-Togo Ranges, Kwahu Ridge, and other isolated ranges, have lower temperatures. Those mountains, however, are not high enough to receive snowfall.

Because the rain-bearing winds originate over the Atlantic Ocean, rainfall is highest along the coast and decreases with distance inland. Heaviest rain occurs in the Axim area in southwestern Ghana. Here, an average of 85 to 90 inches (216–229 centimeters) of rain falls each year. Rainfall decreases gradually northwards to between 40 and 50 inches (102–127 centimeters) each year in the extreme north. The area near the national capital, Accra, receives little rainfall. During the wet season, rainfall is usually very heavy. Continuous heavy rain for three or four days is quite common. This usually produces excessive flooding that can be very destructive. Every year, dozens of people die and property losses resulting from floods runs into billions of *cedis*, the local currency.

Accra has a serious flooding problem. Two reasons account for this: one is the result of physical geography and another is due to human geography. Accra is a low-lying city. Torrential rains, falling during a short period of time, can cause severe flooding. Human activity, on the other hand, also adds to the problem. People dump household garbage and other trash into drains and streams. Choked drains cannot carry excess water away. Additionally, poor building practices cause problems. People build haphazardly, blocking natural drainage lines; they also often build in low-lying, flood-prone areas. To solve this problem, the government is demolishing some of these houses, removing trash from drains, and building new drainage lines.

Wildfires are very common during the February and March dry season. They can be dangerous and very devastating. For example, in 1983 wildfires swept through nearly the entire country. They destroyed cacao farms, food crops, homes, and entire villages. Along the main highways, smoke was everywhere. Many farmers lost their entire harvests, including all of their food. The fires resulted in a major food shortage crisis that affected nearly all of the country. Farmers in Ghana still remember that day, March 3, 1983.

In the past ten years, drought has also been a major problem. The total amount of rainfall received in the country appears to be decreasing. This affects farmers who then have poor yields. It also poses a major problem for the production of electricity. The Akosombo Dam, on the Volta River, is the major source of electricity in Ghana. To operate efficiently, the water level in the lake must be 278 feet (85 meters). Production of hydroelectricity drops to almost nothing when the water level falls below 248 feet (76 meters). When the water is low, less electricity is produced, thereby affecting both industries and people. In 1997–1998, when the water level at the dam dropped to only 237 feet (72 meters), Ghana suffered a major energy crisis. In many places, power was available only 12 hours during each 24-hour period, plunging many people into darkness and making them unable to use many conveniences that so many of us take for granted.

People throughout much of the world have become dependent upon cheap, reliable electrical energy. When the power goes out, it is not possible to listen to a stereo or watch television. Microwave ovens and electric stoves cannot be used. Food in refrigerators may go bad and have to be thrown away. Industrial production is severely affected. For example, an ice cream factory will be able to produce only half of the time. This, of course, means that the price of ice cream increases. Ghanaian children in the cities affected experienced these and many more difficult conditions. Yet, rural families, who do not depend on electricity, were not inconvenienced. They cooked their meals on firewood as always, but they did find that the cost of many products increased as a result of the severe drought conditions.

SOILS, VEGETATION, AND ANIMAL LIFE

Natural vegetation depends mainly on soil and climate. Within limits, humans can create special conditions to grow plants in places not naturally suited for planting. Irrigation is a good example. Such human-induced vegetation is different from what would be expected under conditions of prevailing climate and soil type. Thus, it is possible to transform dry, brown landscapes into green fertile plains through applications of irrigation and fertilizer.

Human activities also affect the natural vegetation. Such factors as the farming method (how land is prepared for planting, how frequently the vegetation is burned or cleared by some other means, and cropping practices) all impact the vegetation. Finally, the past history of land use in an area and the various conditions that have prevailed there also affect the natural vegetation.

Boundaries between vegetation zones or regions are rarely sharp or sudden. Usually, one type smoothly merges into another. Sometimes, a different type of vegetation may emerge as an "island" within an area dominated by another vegetation type. For example, in areas dominated by grass-land, forests may appear on the fringes of rivers or streams. This explains the presence of green oases in parched, brown desert environments.

Throughout Ghana, temperatures are high enough to support plant growth year-round. As a result, the amount and distribution of rainfall is the major factor affecting vegetation. The influence of soils on Ghana's vegetation is rather small. Differences in terrain are minor, hence, elevation and exposure to sunlight play a minor role in vegetation patterns. Also, much of the natural vegetation has been cleared for agriculture, but such trees as the giant kapok, or "silk cotton" trees, valuable

African mahogany, and widespread cedar are still present in the tropical forest zone of the south.

Native animal life has also been reduced drastically, especially in the south, but it remains relatively diverse. Among today's animal species are the leopard, hyena, buffalo, elephant, wild hog, antelope, and monkey. Many species of reptiles are found, including the deadly cobra and the constricting python. Birds and insects abound, as they do elsewhere in the tropical environment.

Ghana's natural vegetation may be divided into four main types or regions. These are: evergreen rain-forest, savanna woodland, coastal scrub and grassland, and strand (land bordering water) and mangrove.

RAIN FOREST

Dense rain forests, with towering trees and a thick blanket of crown foliage, cover nearly all of southwest Ghana. East of Volta River, in the mountainous Togo Ranges, an outlying continuation of this forest emerges as an island. This area has annual rainfall ranging between 50 to 85 inches (127 to 216 centimeters) with two peaks. The first occurs in May–June and the second in October. December to February and July to early September are much drier than the rest of the year.

A large variety of plants, arranged in a series of well-marked layers, characterize the rain forest. Near the ground, especially where the sunlight penetrates to the ground, small herbs and shrubs dominate. Trees with low branches and heavy crowns comprise the second layer that reaches to a height of 60 feet (18 meters). Next, trees with tall, straight stems and relatively small crowns reaching up to 130 feet (40 meters) form the next layer. Finally, very tall trees, some towering to 200 feet (61 meters), form the next layer. These tall trees are increasingly few and far between, because they are widely sought by loggers.

Unlike the relatively homogenous stands of trees found in

the United States, Ghana's rain forest offers a vast array of different plant species. This diversity makes economic exploitation difficult. Moreover, large areas of forest must be destroyed to harvest one large, commercially valuable tree such as mahogany. A road has to be constructed through the forest to reach the chosen tree. When it is felled, the falling tree pulls down nearby trees while falling on others and crushing them. Logging in Ghana's forest can, therefore, be very wasteful and destructive. To extract one tree, many plants are destroyed, although perhaps unintentionally.

The rain forest, for the most part, is evergreen year-round and few trees shed their leaves during the brief dry season in the area with annual rainfall of 70 inches (178 centimeters) or higher. In the areas with less rainfall, the forest becomes semideciduous. A much larger proportion of the trees, particularly those in the two uppermost layers, lose their leaves during the dry season. However, the trees do not all shed all their leaves at once. Thus, the forest always has some barren or dead leaves during this time. Interestingly, the lower layers of trees continue to remain green even in the dry season.

The richness and luxuriant beauty of the forest fades with decreasing rainfall. In the extreme north and east, where rain forest merges with savanna grassland and scrub woodland, rainfall is much lower, and the drying effect of the harmattan is more increased. Vegetation here is heavily influenced by frequent, deliberate burning done in association with hunting and clearing land for farming. Through time, repeated use of fire favors a tall grassland and woody scrubland vegetation, with trees being of species that are fire-resistant.

Many forest reserves are scattered through this vegetation region. The most famous is the Kakum National Park and Conservancy. It is a major tourist attraction and provides a home for many nearly extinct plants and animals. Kakum has over 100 species of mammals, 300 species of birds, and 600 species of butterflies along with elephants, monkeys, and more.

The famous canopy walkway is a very exciting adventure. Consisting of seven hanging bridges high in the treetops, the canopy walk is an incredible experience, but not for the weak of heart. Held up by sturdy ropes and wires attached to trees, the bridges are more than 80 feet (24 meters) above ground. There are four rainforest canopies (tree crowns) in the world that can compare to Kakum in terms of grandeur, but Kakum surpasses them all as the tallest.

The rain forest not only provides useful timber and shelter against harmattan winds from the north, it also provides the perfect ecological environment for Ghana's leading agricultural export, cocoa. Grown in Ghana's rainforest region, cacao trees are the source of cocoa that finds its way into many chocolate bars worldwide. This is also where the major food crops, plantain and cassava, are produced. Kolanut trees and palm trees are also very important.

SAVANNA

The vegetation type that covers most of Ghana is the savanna woodland. The whole area north of the rainforest region, covering more than 65,000 square miles (168,750 square kilometers), is filled with this beautiful, parklike, wooded grassland. Short trees, usually widely spaced, intersperse this beautiful green carpet of grass. Depending on the amount of total rainfall, some of the grasses can reach as high as 12 feet (4 meters). Because the dry season is very intense, lasting usually from November to April, wild and man-made fires are quite frequent and widespread. Hunters sometimes set fires to expose the abundant variety of wild animals that live in this region. Farmers also use fire to clear vegetation from land on which they want to plant crops or herd livestock.

The trees show a remarkable degree of adaptation to the semi-aridity and frequent burning. Many of them are fire-resistant and have thick barks. The strange-looking baobab tree, for example, can withstand long droughts, strong winds, and fire. Its umbrella-shaped crown insulates it from the relatively hostile environment.

The savanna region is Ghana's grain belt. Corn, guinea corn, and millet are favorite crops. Cassava, peanuts, cotton, pepper, tomatoes, beans, and okra are also grown here. Cattle rearing is more important here than anywhere else in Ghana. The drier north is free from tsetse flies. This insect, common throughout much of tropical Africa, causes deadly sleeping sickness in humans. This same disease is called *ngana* disease in cattle. Other animals kept in this region include sheep, goats, chickens, and guinea fowls. They are kept either as pets or food, usually both. Dogs and cats also roam the streets, freely. Unlike laws in the United States, leashing animals at all times is not required. Ghana is like an open petting zoo at times, but always offers nature at its best.

COASTAL SCRUB AND GRASSLAND

This vegetation zone consists of dense scrub with very little grass. Palm trees are common in the moister areas. Giant termite mounds, often 10 feet (3 meters) high or more, are very common. Coconut farming is also common along the beaches. Vegetable gardening and pineapple production are the major activities in this vegetation region.

STRAND AND MANGROVE

This type of vegetation occurs in the immediate coastal area. Plant cover does not form a continuous carpet, but rather a cover of creeping herbs and grasses. Mangrove, with its stilt-like system of roots, dominates the lagoons and lagoon beds.

RIVER SYSTEMS AND LAKES

The Volta is Ghana's longest river. With a total length of about 1,000 miles (1,609 kilometers), it is the largest and most important river in the country. It begins as the Black Volta

Lake Volta was created when the Akosombo Dam was built on the Volta River in 1964. The lake provides water for the dam's hydroelectric plant which supplies Ghana's electric power. Lake Volta is important for transportation as well as fish farming, irrigation, and tourism.

in Burkina Faso, forms the boundary between the northern Ghana and Côte d'Ivoire, and enters the sea through a huge delta. In 1964, the Akosombo Dam was built on the Volta River forming the massive Volta Lake. The Volta feeds the enormous lake, which in turn feeds the hydroelectric dam of Akosombo.

Lake Volta extends 250 miles (402 kilometers) north of the dam and covers 3,275 square miles (8,482 square kilometers). The power station at Akosombo Dam uses water from Lake Volta to generate electric power for Ghana. Lake Volta provides most of Ghana's electricity, and is an important route of inland transportation. It is also a potentially valuable resource for irrigation, fish farming, and tourism.

Other major river systems in Ghana include the Pra, Ankobra, Tano, and Densu. The Pra is the easternmost and the largest of these streams. In the past, it was used extensively to float timber to the coast for export. The Ankobra has a relatively small drainage basin. Small canoes can navigate about 50 miles (80 kilometers) inland from its mouth. It was used to transport machinery to the gold mining region near Tarkwa. The Tano River flows south and empties into a lagoon in the southeast corner of Côte d'Ivoire. It forms part of the border between Ghana and Côte d'Ivoire. East of the Pra, the two most important rivers are the Densu and Ayensu. These rivers provide water for the cities of Accra and Winneba, respectively.

Ghana also has one large natural lake, Lake Bosumtwi, located about 21 miles (34 kilometers) south east of Kumasi, the second largest city. It occupies the cavity formed when the top of a volcano blew off. Its steep-sided walls remind the many tourists of what this really is, a caldera of a former volcano (similar in origin and form to Crater Lake National Park in Oregon). It is about 20 square miles (52 square kilometers) wide and between reaches a depth of 240 feet (73 meters). Lake Bosumtwi's scenic beauty attracts many tourists.

ENVIRONMENTAL CONCERNS

Although Ghana is a beautiful country, full of wonderful resources, it has a number of environmental concerns. Drought severely affects agricultural activities, particularly in the north. Due to excess demand for farmland and logging, deforestation has become a serious concern. In areas where cattle grazing is a major activity, overgrazing is an important issue. Animals graze until there is no vegetation left. Such exposed land suffers erosion. Ghana's wildlife population also is threatened by poaching and habitat destruction. In fact, few elephants remain in Ghana today. Considering all that it has endured through the centuries, however, Ghana's physical environment is in remarkably good condition.

A PLEASANT AND VARIED LANDSCAPE

Ghana, the land of gold, is also the land of green forests, blue skies, and unlimited sunshine. The fine coastal location contributes to warm weather and steady showers, making Ghana's green environment naturally beautiful. Volta Lake contributes electricity and fish, and has great potential for irrigation, agriculture, and tourism. The fertile soils support many crops, including cocoa and pineapples. The natural rain forests contain many nearly extinct species making it a haven for ecotourists.

The Portuguese, who came to Ghana in 1471 to search for gold, built the Elmina Castle in 1482 to protect their interests in ivory, gold, and pepper. Later, the castle was used as a holding center for slaves before their shipment to the United States. The slave trade was stopped in the nineteenth century, but not before as many as 20 million Africans had been enslaved.

3

Ghana
Through Time

G hana has an incredible past and a very long, rich, and detailed oral history. Its historical journey begins perhaps 40,000 years ago and reaches a dynamic present overflowing with optimism. In between, it tells the story of culture change, slavery, battles (including one led by a woman), the fight for self-rule, and much more. In this chapter, the country's fascinating history, from the ancient Gold Coast to modern-day Ghana, will be surveyed.

ANCIENT HISTORY

The earliest evidence of human life in Ghana dates back about 40,000 years. During more recent times, archeological evidence suggests that the area experienced the early Bronze Age (around 4,000 B.C.). Ancestors of some Ghanaians migrated from the north and east. These migrations resulted from the rise and fall of a series of large states in what is now modern West Africa (Ghana, Mali, and Songhai).

Ancient Ghana was one of the best-organized states in the region. Its rulers were known for their wealth in gold, their elaborate palaces and courts, and their military skills. The region's gold mines attracted merchants and rulers of North Africa and the Mediterranean to participate in a very brisk trade. When the Ghana Empire fell in the eleventh century, many of the nobles migrated to modern Ghana to establish new states and to continue trading.

The trans-Saharan trade promoted contacts with peoples in northern, modern Ghana and in the forest to the south. Muslim traders, for example, traded vigorously with the ancestors of the Akan-speaking peoples of southern Ghana. Early Akan states, located on the trade route to the goldfields in the forest zone of the south, benefited tremendously from this trade. Salt and gold were the most important trade items. In fact, between the eleventh and seventeenth centuries, Asante was the world's leading supplier of gold and provided almost two-thirds of the world's supply of the precious metal. Later, the trade broadened to include a wide variety of products. Forest and coastal regions had items, such as kola nuts, salt, and gold, that were needed in the dry north. Similarly, shea butter (obtained from shea tree nuts) and other products from the north were needed in the forest zone. Thus, the north and the south were complementary. Later, new crops such as sorghum, bananas, and cassava were introduced. By the beginning of the sixteenth century, many states in Ghana had become very rich through this trade.

Muslims migrated as scribes and medicine men, and also played a significant role in the trade that linked southern and northern Ghana. Islamic influence dominated in the north, but most Ghanaians retained their traditional animistic religious beliefs. The Muslim-influenced states included Gonja, Mamprusi, and Dagomba. Other tribal states in the region of modern Ghana were the Sisala, Kasena, Kusase, and Talensi, who were mainly farmers.

Of the components that would later make up Ghana, the state of Asante has the most cohesive history and has exercised the greatest influence. The Asante are members of the Twi-speaking branch of the Akan people. Under a series of militant leaders, such as Osei Tutu, they established a huge empire with its capital at Kumasi. The Asante Empire became the most powerful state in the central forest zone.

Okomfo Anokye, the high priest, is said to have caused a stool of gold to descend from the sky. While stools were traditional symbols of authority and rule, the golden stool represented the united spirit of all the allied states and the confederacy of Asante. The Golden Stool remains a respected national symbol of Asante history and figures extensively in festival celebrations and rituals. By the mid-eighteenth century, Asante was a highly organized state that ruled the northern states of Mamprusi, Dagomba, and Gonja. Contact with the coastal Fante, Ga-Adangbe, and Ewe peoples was infrequent and often hostile.

The Portuguese, in 1471, were the first Europeans to arrive on the Gold Coast. They came in search of gold and discovered an abundance of gold wealth among the Asante kings and the Akan people. In fact, they found so much gold between the rivers Ankobra and Volta that they named the place *La Mina*, meaning "the Mine." To protect this prosperous trade in gold, ivory, and pepper they built the first permanent trading post, Elmina Castle, in 1482.

The real wealth, however, came later from a different source, "human gold," or slaves. Due to the high demand in the Americas, trade in slaves soon overshadowed gold as the principal export of the area. Indeed, the West Coast of Africa became the principal source of slaves for the New World. The huge profits to be made from slavery attracted many other Europeans to the Gold Coast. The Dutch, British, and Danes came in the late sixteenth century. For the next 250 years, the European powers fought among themselves over the profitable trade of the Gold Coast. Forts were built, abandoned, attacked, captured, sold, and exchanged.

For example, when the Portuguese lost Elmina to the Dutch in 1642, they left the Gold Coast permanently. By the nineteenth century, when slavery was outlawed, there were 76 forts spread around the coast, averaging about one every 4 miles (6.4 kilometers). The forts were used to store the pillaged gold and slaves until they were shipped to Europe. The average yearly "take" in slaves from what is now Ghana was about 10,000 people.

How many slaves total were taken from West Africa? It is difficult to tell because estimates vary. Overall, an estimated 6.3 million slaves were shipped from West Africa to North and South America. That was not all; many more people died of gunshot and other wounds during slaving raids. In fact, some estimates suggest that Africa lost between 15 and 20 million people through slavery.

The living conditions of the slaves were terrible. In shackles, they were packed into dark and poorly ventilated dungeons with no toilet facilities. Many died of diseases while in captivity awaiting shipment. They were lonely and sad.

One can only wonder what Ghana would be like today had all of those wonderful human resources not been lost as a result of people being carried away as slaves. Could Ghana have become a rich country like the United States? What would the United States be like today had slavery never happened?

Through conquest or purchase, the British had gained possession of all coastal forts by the early nineteenth century. This made them the dominant European power on the Gold Coast. To reinforce their position, they signed various treaties with the local chiefs. The Asante benefited greatly from these arrangements and began to expand their empire. This included invasion of the coastal states such as Fante and Ga. The Asante regarded British domination of the Gold Coat as illegitimate and resisted it with their military might. In the Battle of Nsamankow in 1824, the British governor, Sir Charles MacCarthy, was killed and the British were humiliated.

The British grew more and more uncomfortable with the wealth and influence of the Asantes. These coastal invasions were disrupting trade. To settle the Asante problem permanently, the British invaded Asante with a sizable military force in 1874. They occupied and burned Kumasi, the Asante capital. In 1896, the British again occupied Kumasi and forced Asante to become a protectorate of the British Crown. The position of *Asantehene* (King of the Asantes) was abolished. The king, Nana Prempeh, was arrested and exiled to the Seychelles Islands in the Indian Ocean.

It was during this crisis that Yaa Asantewaa, a queen of the Asantes, emerged as a mighty warrior to mobilize and lead the men in war against the British. The chiefs were discussing how to fight the British and force them to bring back the Asantehene. Yaa Asantewaa saw that some of the chiefs were afraid. Some said that there should be no war. They should rather go to beg the Governor to bring back the Asantehene, Nana Prempeh. Then, suddenly, Yaa Asantewaa stood up and spoke these words:

> Now I have seen that some of you fear to go forward to fight for our king. If it were in the brave days of Osei Tutu, Okomfo Anokye, and Opoku Ware, chiefs would not sit down to see their king taken away without firing a shot. No white man could have dared to speak to chiefs of the Asante the way the Governor spoke to you chiefs this morning. Is it true that the bravery of the Asante is no more? I cannot believe it. It cannot be! I must say this: if you the men of Asante will not go forward, then we will. We the women will. I shall call upon my fellow women. We will fight the British. We will fight till the last of us falls in the battlefields.

Her speech electrified the men. Led by Yaa Asantewaa for months, they fought valiantly and kept the British in the fort.

This painting illustrates the Asante war of 1874.The British were the dominant European power in Ghana, then known as the Gold Coast, during the nineteenth century. They resented the power and influence of the Asante Empire. To eliminate Asante disruption of their trade, the British attacked in force in 1874 and burned Kumasi, the Asante capital.

However, British reinforcements totaling 1,400 soldiers was more than they could handle. Yaa Asantewaa and other leaders were captured and sent into exile. She died in exile, but lives on as a national heroine: the woman who led the men into a major battle against the British.

After the victory, the British proclaimed Asante a colony controlled by the British governor of the Gold Coast. Later, Britain extended its control to include the territories north of Asante. The Volta Region, which lies along the eastern boundary of modern Ghana, was formerly part of a German colony called Togoland. After the defeat of Germany in World War I, Togoland was divided between the British and the French. British Togoland chose to become part of the Gold Coast in a referendum a year before Ghana became independent.

The British administered the Gold Coast through indirect rule. Existing political structures were maintained. Kings and chiefs retained their position, but became representatives of the British who delegated responsibilities to them. Because of this arrangement, some traditional rulers became unpopular in the eyes of their people. Early efforts to seize all "unoccupied lands" along coastal Ghana for the British Crown were fiercely resisted. By World War I, the Gold Coast was the most prosperous and successful colony in all of Africa. It had the best schools and civil service, a cadre of progressive lawyers, and a flourishing press. Still, considerable bitterness existed toward the British.

The main purpose of colonialism was to secure markets for British manufactured goods and to extract resources for British industry. To accomplish this, assisted by the chiefs, the British established a significant infrastructure. In 1901, they constructed the first railway line from Sekondi, on the coast, to the gold mining center of Tarkwa. In 1904, the railway line was extended to Kumasi, the Asante capital, heart of the forest belt and a major logging center.

By 1919, the Gold Coast had roughly 1,200 miles (1,931 kilometers) of motor roads. Commerce flourished and a formal currency (the Gold Coast Pound) was introduced. Palm oil, palm kernel, coconuts, timber, cotton, and rubber were the major exports. Cacao was introduced in 1879. By 1910, it had become the leading export crop. In fact, the Gold Coast had become the world's leading cacao producer with about two-thirds of all production. Many peasant farmers became very rich producing cacao.

To provide labor for offices, the colonial government established schools. Christian missionaries also established schools and provided health care. Hungry for more education than could be provided, the natives also established more schools. The colonial government established the Prince of Wales College at Achimota to provide higher education. Many secondary schools were established in Cape Coast. Some graduates of these institutions went to England or the United States for further studies to become lawyers, doctors, and architects.

At the end of World War I in 1918, Gordon Guggisberg, the new governor, embarked on massive infrastructure development. The railway line was extended from Kumasi to Accra, and a new line was established from Tarkwa to Prestea, another gold mining town. Another railway line was built from Kade to Huni Valley to open up new cacao farms and timber-producing areas. A harbor was built at Takoradi to handle shipping of minerals, timber, and cocoa. Telephones were introduced. A large modern hospital was built in Accra. Importantly, the transportation infrastructure was concentrated mainly in the mining, logging, and cocoa-producing areas. This favored the southern part of the country, particularly the area bounded by Accra, Kumasi, and Sekondi-Takoradi. This area is now known as Ghana's Golden Triangle.

In the late 1920s, numerous organizations devoted to regaining African independence began to surface. In 1946, the emerging middle class, joined by chiefs and the educated elites, formed the first political party, the United Gold Coast Convention (UGCC). Their goal was to work for self-government in the shortest possible time. In 1947, Dr. Kwame

Nkrumah, secretary-general of the UGCC, broke away from the group to form a new party, the Convention People's Party (CPP). This party targeted the common person and particularly the uneducated. Its motto was "Self-Government Now."

CPP was a whirlwind sensation. In 1948, a demonstration to express grievances turned into a riot in which 29 people died. The government blamed, arrested, and imprisoned Kwame Nkrumah and five UGCC leaders. In 1949, Nkrumah called a nationwide strike to force the colonial government to grant independence. The British reacted by promptly imprisoning him again, only to release him two years later. This made Nkrumah a national hero.

In 1957, independence finally arrived. Ghana became the first black African state to win freedom from its colonizers. However, independence did not bring the desired stability or prosperity. Rather, it ushered in a quarter century of economic decline. Between 1966 and 1981, Ghana endured six governments. Two brief civilian governments in 1969 and 1979 were sandwiched between four military governments. Political instability and economic mismanagement took a severe toll on the country. In May 1979, amid severe food shortages, a group of young military officers led by Flight Lieutenant Jerry Rawlings overthrew the government and began a "house-cleaning exercise." They executed several senior military officers and three former heads of state.

Three months later, Rawlings' Armed Forces Revolutionary Council handed over power to a civilian government, only to retake control by force two years later and embark on a Marxist revolution. In 1983, amidst severe food shortages and a severely crippled economy, the Rawlings government changed course midstream and accepted an International Monetary Fund/World Bank-imposed structural adjustment. After ruling Ghana for 19 years, the Rawlings government was defeated in a general election in 2000. The new government, under President John Kufour is taking bold steps to address the economic

In a 1957 ceremony held in Ghana's Parliament House, representatives of the Queen of England read the document that granted freedom from Great Britain. Ghana, which had been working for its freedom for nearly 40 years, was the first African country to gain independence from colonial rule.

problems. Political stability seems to have finally returned. Ghanaians are beginning to hope again. Ghana's economy is inching its way toward stability. The country has also solidified its commitment to democracy. Ghana's story continues to change, but is improving daily.

This is the story of Ghana: gold, colonialism, slavery, independence, chaos, and finally, hope. Ancient Ghana fell, but its name and reputation endured. In 1957, when leaders of the former British colony of the Gold Coast sought an appropriate name for their newly independent state, they named it after ancient Ghana. The choice was more than merely symbolic because modern Ghana, like its namesake, was equally famed for its wealth and trade in gold. Ghana has a golden past, and it looks ahead to what it hopes to be a golden future.

Drums are imperative to music making. They send messages of happiness, sorrow, war, and other themes with meaning being conveyed by the way the drum is beaten.

CHAPTER

4

Ghana's
People and
Cultural Diversity

G
hana has a rich cultural heritage that varies by region and ethnic group. This chapter focuses upon the rich variety of Ghanaian culture. It will explain the beautiful kente cloth and its symbolism, show how to pick a Ghanaian name, and share the recipe for making a Ghanaian favorite dish, peanut butter soup. The languages and the population distribution will also be studied.

POPULATION AND SETTLEMENT

In 2002, Ghana's total population was estimated at 19.36 million and growing at a rate of 2.6 percent per year. This is one of the lowest growth rates in Africa. In the past, Ghanaian women had many children. It was common for one woman to have eight or even ten children. The average number of children that each woman has during her lifetime is called the "fertility rate." So it can be said that

Ghana, like other African countries, had a very high fertility rate. In 1978, the fertility rate was 6.5, but by 2001, it had fallen to 3.82. Compared to the United States with a rate of about 2.1, Ghanaian women continue to have what some people believe to be too many children.

Why do they have so many children? There are several reasons. First, most Ghanaians are small-scale farmers. Because they need help with work on the cacao farms, they have many children. Also, many children die before their first birthday due to childhood diseases and poor health care. The number of children out of 1,000 who die before their first birthday is called the "infant mortality rate." In 2001, almost 57 of every 1,000 children born in Ghana died before their first birthday. In 1957, this figure was more than twice as high. In the United States, in 2002, only seven children per 1,000 die before their first birthdays. Due to the high infant mortality, it made sense for Ghanaians to have many children.

Finally, Ghanaians loved to have many children because those children grew up to be adults who took care of their parents. There was no social security for old people. In fact, Ghanaian culture expects children to provide generously for their parents during their old age and especially to give them a grand funeral. As they say in Ghana, "Because your parents took care of you when you were cutting your teeth, you have to take care of them when their teeth are falling out."

Population density expresses the total number of people per square mile of land. In 2000, Ghana's population density was about 212 people per square mile. Southern Ghana has a higher population density than the northern part. The highest population density is in the "Golden Triangle." This is the area between Accra, the national capital, Kumasi, the second largest city, and Takoradi in the Western Region.

Ghana's largest city, Accra, has about 1.5 million people. The second largest city, Kumasi, has about 800,000. Most people, however, live in small rural settlements. In fact, about 60 percent of the country's population is rural. Generally speaking, population density decreases the farther northward one goes. This is partially explained by the fact that southern Ghana is more economically developed than the north.

The country is divided into 10 administrative regions: Northern, Upper West, Upper East, Volta, Ashanti, Western, Eastern, Central, Brong-Ahafo and Greater Accra. The population distribution for these administrative regions is presented in Table 2.

REGION	POPULATION	MALE	FEMALE	CAPITAL
Western	1,842,878	925,708	917,170	Takoradi
Central	1,580,047	753,053	826,994	Cape Coast
Greater Accra	2,909,643	1,433,093	1,476,550	Accra
Volta	1,612,299	775,257	837.042	Ho
Eastern	2,108,852	1,034,922	1,073,930	Koforidua
Ashanti	3,187,601	1,556,587	1,631,014	Kumasi
Brong Ahafo	1,824,822	913,035	911,787	Sunyani
Northern	1,854,994	921,138	933,856	Tamale
Upper East	917,251	437,245	480,006	Bolgatanga
Upper West	573,860	274,981	298,879	Wa

Source: Ghana Statistical Service, 2000 Census (Provisional figures)

Table 2. Ghana's Population Distribution

Compared to Americans, Ghanaians die at a very young age. The average number of years a person is expected to live is called "life expectancy." In Ghana, life expectancy in 2002 was about 57 years, compared to 77 years in the U.S. At the time of independence, however, life expectancy was only 44 years, so there has been much improvement. In fact, Ghana's life expectancy today is among the highest in Africa.

RELIGION

Ghanaians are very religious and their beliefs permeate every aspect of daily life. The imprint of religion seems to be everywhere. It is a part of everyday speech, and it appears in the names of businesses. Ask a person, "How are you?" and most will answer, "By God's grace I am fine." This is the proper response whether or not a person is devoutly religious. Scanning the phone book's Yellow Pages for the names of businesses also will attest to the importance of religion. Some of this author's favorites include: "Jesus Saves Catering," "God Will Provide Auto Shop," and "My Redeemer Pharmacy." The all-time favorite, however, is "Holy Bar," a tavern selling beer and hard liquor. Passenger vehicles are not exempt. They also carry religious signs such as "Faith," "God Never Mistakes," and "Psalm 23."

Even before the Europeans arrived, Ghanaians worshipped what to them was an Almighty God, Onyame, who created everything. However, Onyame was too holy to be approached by mere mortals, so lesser gods, spirits, and deities were the intermediaries between Onyame and humans. These spirit beings could inhabit natural phenomena such as lakes, rivers, mountains, trees, and even huge rocks.

Dead ancestors live in this spirit world from which they always watch over the living. Reverence for dead ancestors was very important, because they had the power to bring misfortune upon the living. In fact, sickness, accidents, and even death had spiritual explanations. Sacrifices were regularly offered to appease the ancestral spirits and ask for their blessing. During festivals and celebrations, ritualistic pouring and offering drinks to ancestors and praying for their blessing are major activities reserved for the elite.

In Ghana today, Christianity, Islam, and animism (indigenous beliefs) are the major religions. Christianity is the leading religion, with 69 percent of Ghanaians claiming Christian ties.

Religious beliefs are very important to the Ghanaian people. Religion even reaches into business names such as the "God First Haircut" barbershop. Similar religion-related names can be found among all types of business establishments and services.

Muslims (followers of the Islamic faith) make up 16 percent of the population. The remaining hold traditional animistic beliefs, or claim no religious ties. The exact number of Muslims in Ghana has been a topic of hot debate recently. The *CIA World Fact Book* incorrectly states that 38 percent of Ghanaians follow traditional animistic religions, 30 percent are Muslims, 24 percent are Christians, and 8 percent comprise other religions. This figure has been quoted widely, but it is inaccurate. According to the 2000 Census, Muslims comprised 15.6 percent of Ghana's population, while Christians constitute 69 percent. The Director of Ghana's census questioned the CIA claim and affirmed that it has no basis. This makes sense because Muslims dominate in the northern part of the country, a very sparsely populated region. In contrast, Christianity dominates in the southern, more densely populated region.

Religious beliefs in Ghana affect every area of daily activity. Important life events such as birth, reaching adulthood, childbearing (for women), and death are highly ritualized. In order to maintain balance, the roles of chiefs within the state, elders within the lineage, and priests within society are crucial. Religious roles are demonstrated during festivals when people are organized into activities that renew and strengthen relations with ancestors.

Funerals are profoundly creative and colorful community celebrations. They involve a lot of drumming, dancing, and symbolism. Black, red, and brown are colors symbolizing mourning and are the colors that are preferred at funerals. For Christian funerals, white is frequently used. The explanation is that the deceased is going to heaven, so the funeral is a time to rejoice. Funerals tend to be very expensive and elaborate. The poorest and most divided of families usually secure enough funds to provide a decent ceremony even if it puts them in debt. If the living fail to give the dead a fitting funeral, the survivors will be plagued with misfortune sent from the dead. This could include sickness and even death. Consequently, special clothing and even calendars commemorating the dead are produced and distributed. In Southern Ghana, particularly in Accra, special coffins indicating the profession of the individual are used. A pilot will be buried in a casket shaped like an airplane, a fisherman may be buried in a fish-shaped casket, and a driver may be buried in an automobile-shaped casket.

LANGUAGE AND ETHNICITY

Ghana is highly diverse in terms of ethnicity and language. Its principal ethnic groups are the Akans (Twi- and Fante-speaking), Guans, Ewes, Dagombas, Gas, Gonjas, Dagabas, Walas, and Frafras. The Akan, comprising 44 percent of the population, are found in south-central Ghana and the western coastal regions. Moshi-Dagomba, comprising 16 percent, live in northern and upper regions. The Ewe, comprising 13 percent of the population, are mainly concentrated in the Volta Region, while the Ga (8 percent) live mainly in the Greater Accra region. The Akan, Moshi-Dagomba, Ewe, and Ga tribes are all named after their languages.

Linguistically, it seems odd that English is the official language of Ghana. Twi, Fante, Ga, Hausa, Dagbani, Ewe, and Nzema are the major languages, but the official language is the language of the colonial master, Great Britain. This is a direct result of colonialism. It also explains why French-speaking countries surround Ghana. With so many languages to choose from at independence, it made sense to choose a neutral one: English. Of course, speaking English was also a sign of modernity. Today, English is the medium of instruction, even in primary school.

OTHER ASPECTS OF GHANAIAN CULTURE

Over the course of time, Ghanaians have developed a rich, beautiful culture that compares to no other. Religion is as important as language, but there is so much more to appreciate about Ghanaian culture, including its unique architecture, music, theatre, traditions, and cuisine. All of these cultural elements provide Ghana with a wonderful sense of diversity, as will be shown in the following section.

Kente cloth is perhaps Ghana's most unique cultural contribution. The celebrated icon of African cultural heritage around the world, kente is identified by its dazzling, multi-colored patterns of bright colors, geometric shapes, and bold designs. It is very popular among African Americans in the United States today, but the kente cloth is Ghanaian in origin. Kente is a ceremonial cloth hand woven on a treadle loom. Strips measuring about four inches wide are sewn together into larger pieces of cloth. Cloths come in various colors, sizes, and designs and are worn during very important social and religious occasions. In a cultural context, kente is more important than just a cloth. It is a visual interpretation of history, philosophy, ethics, oral literature, moral values, social code of conduct,

Kente cloth is woven on a traditional treadle loom and is Ghana's most important cultural contribution. As a special cloth with a variety of colors, sizes, and striking patterns, Kente cloth is worn during important social and ceremonial occasions.

religious beliefs, political thought, and artistic principles.

The origins of kente cloth date back to twelfth-century Ghana. Kings, queens, and important figures of state in Asante society wore the cloth during ceremonial events and special occasions. The term "kente" has its roots in the word *kenten*, which means basket, because the cloth somewhat resembles a basket design when woven. The original Asante name of the cloth was *nsaduaso*, or *nwontoma*, meaning "a cloth hand-woven on a loom." It is still used today by Asante weavers and elders. However, the term "kente" is the most popularly used today, in and outside Ghana. One of the most interesting things about this cloth design is that each pattern has its own meaning and color. Here are a few examples:

Nyankonton literally means "God's eyebrow" (the rainbow). It was created in exaltation of the beauty and mystery of the rainbow phenomenon. The arrangement of warped thread mimics the visual characteristics of the rainbow. This cloth symbolizes divine beauty and creativity, gracefulness, unique- ness, and good omen.

Sika Futoro means "gold dust." Before the use of coins and paper as money, gold dust was used as a means of exchange with the Akan peoples. It was therefore considered a symbol of wealth and prosperity. The main use of elaborate textured patterns in yellows, orange, and reds imitates the visual charac- teristics of gold dust. The cloth symbolizes wealth, royalty, elegance, spiritual purity, and honorable achievement.

Aabusua Ye Dom means, "The extended family is a force." Among the Akan people, the extended family is the foundation of society. Like a military force, members of the family are collectively responsible for the material and spiritual well being, the physical protection, and the social security of all its members. The cloth was designed to celebrate and emphasize such positive attributes of the extended family system. In its many variations and background colors, the cloth symbolizes strong family bond, the value of family unity, collective work and responsibility, and cooperation.

A less well-known, but equally impressive textile product of Ghanaian origin is the *adinkra*, a highly valued hand-printed and hand-embroidered cloth. Its origin is traced to the Asante people of Ghana. Around the nineteenth century, the Asante developed their unique art of adinkra printing. *Adinkra* means goodbye. Originally, only the royalty and spiritual leaders wore the cloth, for mourning, during funeral services. It can now be worn by anyone for any occasion. The symbols and their mean- ings are still used to convey a message. The motifs are filled with symbolism and Akan philosophy and wise sayings. Here are a few examples.

ADINKRA MOTIFS AND SYMBOLISM

 Osrane ne nsoroma (moon and star). A symbol of faithfulness.

 Gye Nyame (accept God). Symbol of the omnipotence and immortality of God.

 Odenkyem (crocodile) *"Da nsuo mu nso ohome mframa nye nsuo.* (The crocodile lives in the water, yet it breathes air, not water.)"

 Akoma (the heart). *"Nya akoma* (take heart)." Have patience. Symbol of patience and endurance.

 Aya (the fern). This word also means 'I am not afraid of you.' A symbol of defiance.

MUSIC

Music is an indispensable part of Ghanaian culture. It is present in nearly every activity, including work, play, celebrations, and funerals. Drums are imperative to music making and the "Talking Drum" has been used for communicating messages. In the hands of skilled performers, they can reproduce the sounds of proverbs, or praise songs through a specialized "drum language." Whether accompanying dances or sending messages, the sound of these instruments can carry many miles. They send messages of happiness, sorrow, war, and other themes with meaning being conveyed by the way that the drum is beaten. Ghana is also the home of highlife music, which is enjoyed throughout Africa and the world.

Dancing to Adowa music in the Ashanti region conveys how important drumming and dancing are to Ghanaian culture. Drums are essential for celebrations, work, and play. "Talking drums" can be used for communication and, with talented players, can reproduce the sounds of proverbs or praise songs.

NAMES

Names have special meaning and symbolism in Ghana. A person's name is believed to influence his or her character. Thus, great care and thought go into selecting names for children. Every Ghanaian's name has at least two main parts. The first part is the *kradin* (soul's name). This comes from the day of birth and the baby's gender. A baby born on Friday is called Kofi (male) or Afua (female). Similarly, a baby born on Saturday is called Kwame (male) or Ama (female).

Day of the Week	Male	Female
Sunday	Kwesi	Esi
Monday	Kwadjo	Adwoa
Tuesday	Kwabena	Abena
Wednesday	Kweku	Ekua
Thursday	Yaw	Yaa
Friday	Kofi	Efua
Saturday	Kwame	Ama

Table 3. Ghanaian Day Names

The second part of the name is the *agyadin* (father's name), or the *abusuadin* (family name). This is the name chosen by the child's father, usually from a list of ancestral names of the father's line of descent. Fathers name their children after ancestors that they most admire, particularly those models of commendable behavior. It also may simply be the father's surname. Thus, a name can tell us a lot about the owner of that name. The name Kofi Annan (the United Nations secretary-general who won the Nobel Peace Prize) belongs to a male called Annan who was born on a Friday. Similarly, Ghana's first president, Kwame Nkrumah, was born on a Saturday.

Children are treasured in Ghanaian society. Adult members of the family do everything possible to ensure that the child is raised in a happy and nurturing environment. Each person, young or old, belongs to a large "extended family." Family in Ghana is more than parents and children. It also includes siblings, uncles, cousins, aunts, grandparents, and great grand-relations. This extended family is a source of strength and assurance. In times of difficulty, they share the cost of relief. In times of joy, they celebrate together.

Women have a fascinatingly visible role in Ghanaian society. Besides the traditional role of giving birth to and raising children,

Family is very important in Ghana where "extended family" includes everybody from siblings to great grandparents. In times of joy, the entire family celebrates together. Older family members are highly respected and children are especially treasured.

ancient political systems were dominated by "queenmothers." The queenmother enjoyed significant political powers. The Akan *ohemmaa* obtains her title due to seniority in the royal matrilineage (ancestral descent on the mother's side). She is the embodiment and personification of wisdom. During a jury trial, the expression for jury deliberations to determine a verdict literally translates as "Going to consult the Old Lady."

Unlike the dual inheritance system in the United States, inheritance in Ghana is either patrilineal or matrilineal. A person may inherit from either the father or the mother, but not both. Among the Asante, who are matrilineal, a person inherits from his uncle or mother's brother.

TRADITIONS

Ghanaians like to have fun and celebrate. They also like good food. At any festival, both will most likely be found. Village-specific festivals and events occur throughout the year.

A few Ghanaian traditions or customs include the following.

The 42-day cycle of the Ashanti religious calendar culminates in *Kumasi* (the "City of the Golden Stool") with *Akwasidee*, a public ceremony at the palace involving the main chiefs and priests. The *Aboakyer*, or Deer Hunt Festival, is held in May in Winneba. Elmina's *Bakatue Festival*, celebrating the beginning of the fishing season, is held on the first Tuesday of July with local chiefs parading through town in full regalia, followed by singers, dancers, and stilt walkers. On the first Saturday in September, a raucous carnival called the "Fetu Festival" takes place in Cape Coast, featuring an all-day parade of local chiefs. The Pan-African Historical Theatre Festival (Panafest) is a cultural drama spectacle held throughout Ghana in December of even-numbered years. National holidays include Independence Day on March 6, Republic Day on July 1, and Revolution Day on December 31.

FOOD

Ghanaians like food. They like to make it and they enjoy feeding people who appreciate the food. Fruit is very popular. It usually is picked ripe and sold the same day. Some of the favorites are pineapples, bananas, and mangoes, which are all incredibly sweet with a wonderful flavor because they have been picked at precisely the right time.

One of the main staples in Ghana is rice. Rice is easily stored, cooked, and sold. It makes for a quick meal at any time of the day. In Ghana, the nutritious grain is eaten with stew, eaten fried, eaten with soup, and consumed in just about any other way imaginable. Another popular food in Ghana is called *Fufu*. In fact, if an Akan man has eaten a meal, but it is without Fufu, he will claim he has not eaten!

Fufu consists of cassava, yam, or plantain that has been cooked, pureed, and mashed into a ball. Fufu is an ever-present and much loved staple throughout most of West Africa. It can be topped with a fiery sauce or served as the bland companion to a main dish. Most Ghanaian foods are eaten with a thick, flavor-rich soup. Meals are very filling so that it is not necessary to eat again for many hours.

Here is a delicacy from Ghana—Peanut Butter Soup. This may very well be the strangest and most delicious food ever to come from Ghana.

Chicken Peanut Butter Soup (serves 6 to 8)

Ingredients
8 to 12 chicken pieces
1 cup (250 grams) smooth peanut butter
1 medium onion, chopped
2 quarts (2 liters) warm water
1 teaspoon salt
2 medium ripe tomatoes, peeled or 2 tablespoons tomato paste
1 teaspoon pepper
Diced pimentos, optional
1 teaspoon hot curry powder, optional

Preparation
Add onion and seasonings to the chicken. Moisten with a little water and cook over medium heat in a large saucepan for 15 minutes. Stir once or twice. While the chicken is cooking, mix the peanut butter with water in a bowl until smooth. Add it to chicken. Bring to a boil. Continue boiling for 30 minutes. Grind tomatoes in a blender until smooth. Add the tomato pulp to the soup. Simmer until the chicken is tender and oil begins to form in the soup. Stir from time to time. Sprinkle with pimentos before serving. Accompany with fufu, boiled potatoes, rice or yams. Cooking time: 1 1/2 hours.

Sounds good, doesn't it? Ghana is a land of many cultures, ethnic groups, and traditions that simply add to the wonder of this sunny coastal country. Two of the most important elements of any culture are its government and economic activity. But before moving on to these topics, have you figured out what your Ghanaian name is? It is not difficult. Just find your day of birth and add your surname. Go ahead and try the peanut butter soup. You can then say with pride that you have "visited" Ghana!

Kwame Nkrumah, shown with United Nations Secretary-General Dag Hammarskjöld in 1961, became Ghana's first freely-elected leader in 1957. Educated in Ghana and the United States, Nkrumah was experienced in political organization. He led the country for nine years but was overthrown by the military in 1966.

CHAPTER

5

Politics In Ghana

G hana began as a gold-rich country, the star of Black Africa. It attracted immigrants from many lands, particularly economic refugees. In the 1990s, however, Ghanaians were leaving their own country in massive numbers as economic refugees to distant lands. Today remittances—money sent back home— from Ghanaians abroad are a major source of foreign exchange. How did this happen? How did once wealthy Ghana fall from grace? Could it have been avoided? This chapter will try to answer those questions.

Remember the United Gold Coast Convention (UGCC), the first political party that was established in the Gold Coast to press for political independence? It was formed by the educated elite, the emerging middle class, and a few tribal chiefs. Mr. George Grant, a wealthy businessman, and Dr. J. B. Danquah, a lawyer, led the

UGCC. They advocated self-government at the earliest possible opportunity and pursued a capitalist democratic ideology. In 1946, they invited Dr. Kwame Nkrumah to become the party's permanent secretary. Kwame Nkrumah had studied at Ghana's Prince of Wales College in Achimota, and in the United States at Lincoln University and the University of Pennsylvania. Nkrumah had much experience in political organization and held very strong ideas about African unity.

Unlike the UGCC leadership, Nkrumah wanted "self-government now." If these leaders had agreed, Ghana's history would be entirely different. Unfortunately, they did not. Nkrumah broke away from the UGCC and established his own party, the Convention Peoples' Party. He courted and organized the poorly educated, ordinary people into his party. By promising to transform the Gold Coast into paradise in ten years, Nkrumah's popularity grew. The UGCC was swept aside. For him, political power was the key to Ghana's development. "Seek ye first the political kingdom, and all things will be added with it," he declared. Because his ideas appealed to so many people, Nkrumah easily won the 1957 elections, and his CPP formed Ghana's first government. The UGCC, meanwhile, saw Nkrumah as a traitor and never forgave him.

On attaining independence, Nkrumah set out to build a Ghana that was free from poverty, ignorance, and disease. He wanted to accomplish that overnight. He embarked on several major development projects to make Ghana the star of Africa. For example, a modern four-lane highway was constructed between Tema and Accra at a cost of £2 million (roughly equivalent to $3 million U.S. dollars). A national airline, Ghana Airways, and a national shipping company, Black Star Line, were established. The Akosombo Dam was built to provide hydroelectric power for industrialization. An aluminum smelting project, Volta Aluminum Company (VALCO), was established, although the terms were not favorable for Ghana.

The Kwame Nkrumah University of Science and Technology

was also established to provide training in science, engineering, pharmacy, agriculture, and architecture among other things. Education at all levels was expanded and primary education became compulsory and free. Health services were expanded with many new hospitals and clinics and two teaching hospitals. Postal and telephone services were quickly expanded.

Nkrumah wanted to do it all, to develop Ghana fully and immediately. This is where the problem began. He opted for socialism as a means of catching up quickly with the developed world. He established state farms, employing thousands of people to expand and diversify agricultural production. Experts from socialist countries were invited to help Ghana undertake various development projects. Projects completed with such help included shoe factories, cement factories, a rubber and tire factory, a pharmaceutical complex, and numerous others. Nkrumah maintained that state ownership of production was the main strategy for Ghana's industrialization. He was forcibly removed from power by the military in 1966. Why was this done?

By the early 1960s, Ghana's economy was beginning to show signs of strain. The capital Ghana had gained at independence was gobbled up by the many projects, and new sources of money were limited. Most new industries were not yet profitable. For example, the state farms had too many workers, and suffered from poor management, political interference, and nepotism (favoring relatives). Most of the equipment imported from Eastern European countries was not suitable for Ghana's physical environment. By the time Nkrumah was ousted, more than 60 percent of the machinery imported for state farms was beyond repair.

Moreover, while focusing on state farms, the small-scale farmers who had made Ghana the world's leading cocoa producer were ignored and heavily taxed. The government paid the farmers much less than the world price for cocoa and used the difference to support the massive development programs. Since cocoa production was centered in the Asante region, the Asantes considered this unfair and discriminatory. While foreigners were invited to invest in industry and commercial enterprise, Ghanaians were prohibited from any business other than petty trading. This was done to promote socialism and prevent the emergence of a capitalist class.

These developments enraged the original enemies of Nkrumah, particularly the UGCC, but their opposition was crushed. Some opposition leaders were jailed and others fled into exile. By 1964, Ghana had "chosen" to become a one-party state, the CPP. Corruption, nepotism and discrimination based on party affiliation became widespread. The government also pursued a variety of African unity objectives. A large sum of Ghana's money was spent on supporting other African countries that were fighting for independence.

In 1965, the world price of cocoa fell drastically. Ghana was in deep trouble. It could not pay its debts. Western governments such as the United States, which resented Ghana's ties with socialist countries, including the Soviet Union, refused to help. Basic consumer items such as sugar, flour, soap, milk, drugs, and automobile parts became almost nonexistent. By the beginning of 1966 Ghana had an external debt of £120 million and no foreign exchange. It desperately needed to improve its inefficient industries. Conditions were ripe for a change of government, and this happened on February 24, 1966.

THE NATIONAL LIBERATION COUNCIL (1966–1969)

The military coup, or takeover, of 1966 marked a turning point in Ghana's development history. The new military government, the National Liberation Council (NLC), cited economic chaos, dictatorship, and abuse of human rights as reasons for the coup. However, the underlying reason was Nkrumah's pro-socialist and anti-capitalist policies. Most of the military leadership had been trained at western military

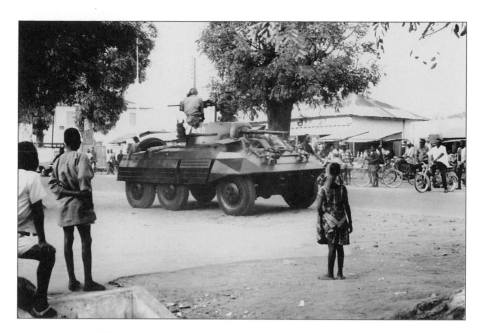

In 1966, the military ousted the pro-Soviet, anti-capitalist Nkrumah government, citing economic chaos, human rights abuses, and dictatorship as the basis for their actions. The new government, called the National Liberation Council, lasted for three years until the elections of 1969.

institutions, particularly in Britain, and resented the anti-West attacks. The economic crisis and political authoritarianism turned the people away from Nkrumah and the CPP. The NLC saw themselves as liberators.

In the three years it held power, the NLC sought to reverse the socialist course of Ghana's development. Instead of socialism, liberal capitalist policies were pursued. Most of the projects having Eastern European support were abandoned. Unfortunately, Ghana still owed the debt that had been incurred on those projects. For example, a gold refinery being built at Tarkwa, that was 90 percent complete and scheduled to open in June 1966, was abandoned. A state fishing complex, built at a cost of £2.3 million, also was abandoned. Its 350 Soviet workers were expelled and its 28 fishing vessels abandoned.

The NLC also encouraged Ghanaians to invest in every part of the economy. State ownership of production was completely discouraged. Ghanaian private ownership was preferred and encouraged over foreign ownership. For example, more construction contracts went to Ghanaians. Also, Ghanaian businesses received preferential treatment in the distribution of import licenses. The currency was devalued 30 percent against the U.S. dollar. The price paid to cacao farmers was increased substantially. Their tax burden was reduced. Of course, they were very happy. Ghanaian businesses were pleased too. The military and police were particularly glad, because their privileges and conditions of service were improved drastically. They received new uniforms, arms, and better barracks.

The NLC actions won approval from western nations, and Ghana's commercial suppliers restored supplies. Debt repayment dates and terms were changed to help the NLC government. Food production, however, continued to suffer. Unemployment soared as workers in government enterprises were laid off. Worried workers embarked on disruptive strikes to demand improved working conditions. These strikes were met with lockouts, dismissals, and brutal police force. Concerned by the strikes, the NLC decreed "incitement to a general strike" as a capital offense punishable by death.

Finally, the NLC took steps to destroy the Nkrumah legacy. The CPP was abolished. Those who had suffered under Nkrumah were embraced. Chiefs who had been appointed under Nkrumah were removed, and those who had been removed by Nkrumah were restored. Before handing over power to a civilian government, the NLC passed several laws to deliberately exclude many CPP politicians and people of socialist leanings from running for political office. The NLC was determined to make sure that Nkrumah and his ideas were dead forever in Ghana.

Among the parties that emerged, two were important: the Progress Party (PP) led by Dr. K. A. Busia, a professor of sociology, and the National Alliance of Liberals (NAL) led by Gbedema, a businessman from the Volta region. The PP was simply a reincarnation of the UGCC. The second republic led by Dr. Busia was inaugurated in October 1969, and the NLC members retired to enjoy their accumulated wealth.

THE SECOND REPUBLIC (1969–1972)

Leadership of the second republic was mainly composed of academic elites and members of the middle class (people rejected by the Nkrumah government). They inherited an economy in recession due to the sudden dismantling of Nkrumah policies and programs. To accommodate the economic realities, the government devalued the currency by 90 percent. It increased interest rates and raised the price of petroleum products. Free medical care established by Nkrumah was abolished, and the prices of basic commodities increased. Free college and university education started by Nkrumah was replaced by a student loan plan that was interest free and payable over 12 years.

The government sought to enhance Ghanaian participation in business and prohibited foreigners from engaging in selected business such as retail trade, road construction, and banking. It enacted a law, the Alien Compliance Order, which ordered all immigrants without valid residence and work permits to leave Ghana. The ruthless enforcement of this order led to the forced expulsion of massive numbers of people from neighboring countries. Most of Ghana's neighbors including Burkina Faso, Côte d'Ivoire, Togo, Mali, Niger, and Nigeria were infuriated. Ghana was also isolated on the African continent because, contrary to the OAU charter, the government sought dialogue with apartheid South Africa.

Rural development was a major priority of this government. It constructed 450 miles (724 kilometers) of feeder (branch transportation) roads in 1970 alone. Rural health centers were expanded and health workers and teachers were assigned to rural areas. In

Accra, the capital, a centralized underground sewer system was planned, but the government was removed from office before the project began. Today, Ghana lacks a centralized sewer system.

These austerity measures created difficult hardships for most people. Widespread unrest involved students, public workers, and former CPP supporters. The military and police were affected most because their gains under the NLC were taken away. Their reaction was swift and decisive; 1972 witnessed another military coup.

THE NATIONAL REDEMPTION COUNCIL AND THE SUPREME MILITARY COUNCIL (1972–1978)

Lt. Col. I. K. Acheampong announced the 1972 coup that brought in the National Redemption Council (NRC) government. Citing the economic difficulties, arbitrary dismissals, and wanton arrests, he said it was time to redeem Ghana from "economic mismanagement and incompetence." Parliament was dissolved, and all political parties were banned. All except one member of the NRC were military. No clear date for return to civilian rule was announced. Army officers were appointed to high positions in government departments and state institutions to replace civilians.

To give a favorable image, the NRC abolished the dialogue with South Africa initiated by the previous government and reaffirmed Ghana's commitment to nonalignment. Relations were resumed with socialist block countries as well as capitalist democratic countries. The NRC blamed the economic crisis on Busia's economic policies. It tried to revive Nkrumah's socialist policies while dismantling the capitalist economic order of the NLC and the Busia government. The devalued currency was revalued by 42 percent, and most workers dismissed by the previous government were reinstated. The price of cocoa was increased and the tax on cocoa was reduced. Social groups that opposed Busia were appeased. Food production was increased by numerous state farms all over the country.

Between 1972 and 1975, the NRC was very popular.

From 1975 to 1979, however, the economy took a dramatic nose dive. There was an acute shortage of foreign exchange. There were few available imported consumer goods. Sharp decreases in critical agricultural and industrial production became rampant. The transport system was in ruins, literally crippling the economy. In Accra, many government workers refused to go to work because of lack of transport. Absenteeism and tardiness were common. Long lines of people waiting for food or transport were seen everywhere. Because of the extremely low value of the currency, many people who lived along the border preferred to use the currency of neighboring countries. As economic refugees, many people left the country for neighboring countries. Smuggling of cocoa and minerals such as gold and diamonds reached unimaginable proportions.

In these extreme difficulties, Acheampong established the Supreme Military Council to administer the country, with himself as chairman. Some new military faces were added to the NRC, and the plunder of Ghana continued. Service conditions of the military and police were again enhanced and new military equipment was imported. Opposition newspapers were banned. In the escalating economic difficulties, survival became the key. Urban workers cultivated their own food and raised poultry in their backyards. Almost everybody was trading something and illegal-trading practices proliferated.

The exodus of Ghanaians continued, particularly the educated and professionals such as physicians and teachers. In a desperate attempt to perpetuate himself in power, Col. Acheampong proposed a tripartite political system comprising the military, the police, and civilians, called Union Government (UNIGOV). A referendum staged by the SMC returned a massive victory for UNIGOV.

To save the country from further embarrassment and deterioration, General Akuffo, a member of the SMC, forced Acheampong out of power in a palace coup. He was put under house arrest. Between 1978 and 1979, the Supreme Military Council II tried to restore sanity into Ghana's economy. The currency was devalued by 58.2 percent, and to control inflation, the currency was changed. Political prisoners were released and a constituent assembly was appointed to draft a new constitution. Ironically, these were the very measures the Busia regime had tried to implement. Unfortunately, it appeared to be too little too late. The stage was set for another coup.

THE ARMED FORCES REVOLUTIONARY COUNCIL (AFRC)

On June 4, 1979, Jerry Rawlings and other junior officers announced the overthrow of the SMC government and the establishment of the AFRC to rule the country. They promised a housecleaning exercise, an end to corruption, and public accountability. The unemployed, students, and impoverished workers cheered them on. On June 16, 1979, General Acheampong and General Utuka were secretly tried for crimes against the people. They were found guilty and executed. Ten days later, another six top military officials, including General Akuffo, also were executed. While these executions received popular support in urban areas, such radical measures were unknown in Ghana and were rejected by rural residents and the elite. Professional associations such as lawyers and doctors asked the AFRC to hand over power to a civilian government.

The AFRC intervened in the market and imposed price controls. Blaming the greed of traders for high prices and shortage of goods, those refusing to sell their products at the ridiculously low government prices were severely punished. Public flogging, as well as stripping and humiliation of female traders, was widespread. Many were jailed for making illegal profits. The largest market in Accra, Makola, was dynamited because it was the center of trade malpractices. Markets in other regional centers suffered the same fate.

Many businessmen were arrested for "economic crimes."

Fearing "revolutionary justice," many "criminals" (those who were relatively rich), fled the country. Some of those who fled were tried in absentia and sentenced to various terms of imprisonment. On September 24, 1979, after 112 days in office, the AFRC handed over power to a civilian government led by Dr. Hilla Limann. The AFRC asked the Limann government to continue the housecleaning exercise and "safeguard the achievements of the AFRC." This was another way of saying, "Please protect us from our enemies."

DR. HILLA LIMANN AND THE PEOPLE'S NATIONAL PARTY (1979–1981)

Dr. Hilla Limann's government was made up of many academics. It claimed the CPP heritage, and President Limann tried to court both socialist and capitalist countries. It promoted a new investment code to encourage both foreign and Ghanaian investment in the economy. The government took too long in taking drastic actions about the national economic crisis, however. The economy continued to struggle. As a democratically elected government, the PNP could not match the "Action Now" politics of the AFRC. Many people quickly became disillusioned. The serious political problems they inherited from the AFRC distracted them and prevented their concentrating on the economy.

The most critical problem was a transitional clause in the constitution that prevented the review of AFRC decisions. This meant that the government could not ensure justice for those who had been tried unfairly and had their life savings, property, and other assets confiscated. Rawlings and his colleagues from the AFRC were discharged from the military and because of their threat, they were placed under surveillance. Rawlings, however, continued to grow in popularity. The continuing economic crisis and shortage of consumer goods provided the framework for another military coup. It happened again on December 31, 1981.

THE PROVISIONAL NATIONAL DEFENSE COUNCIL (1981–1983)

During its first two years, the Provisional National Defense Council (PNDC) government attempted to carry Nkrumah's Marxist ideas to an extreme. At large rallies, people were reminded that Ghana's problems were due to imperialist forces, mainly the United States, Britain, and western capitalism. People were told they were poor because greedy and wicked foreign capitalists and their local allies were exploiting and cheating them. There were only two groups of people, they claimed, the rich and the poor. The only way to ensure peace was for the poor to rise up against their oppressors and demand justice. The PNDC was a friend of the poor, and also friendly with radical socialist countries such as Cuba, Libya, the USSR, and Nicaragua. As usual, projects of the previous government were abandoned. Politicians were arrested. Their property and bank accounts and those of their wives and children were confiscated. All soldiers retired by the previous government were reinstated.

Radical economic measures taken at this time further damaged the economy. The government withdrew all 50 cedi notes (the highest denomination of the currency) from circulation. This hurt rural residents most because they had no access to banks. Their money became worthless. Traders once again were portrayed as being "enemies of the revolution" and flogged or otherwise humiliated publicly for being greedy and making excessive profits. Their goods were seized and sold at ridiculously low prices. Many stores retaliated by refusing to open.

Personal bank account balances of more than 50,000 cedis ($1,250) were frozen and their owners required to account for their wealth. Those who could not do so in a satisfactory manner were forced to forfeit their wealth, and those who could were required to pay excessive "taxes." Special "People's Tribunals" were established to try those accused of economic crimes. No

Flight Lieutenant Jerry Rawlings, shown here addressing a crowd, led a military coup in 1981 after years of economic decline and government changes. The Rawlings government, called the Provisional National Defense Council, was Marxist. It was unable to keep the economy from plunging into even greater depths.

appeals were allowed. Arbitrary arrests, detention without trial, and other human rights abuses were common. Because state policy was so arbitrary, many people fled the country.

By 1982, the economy was in shambles. Hunger was widespread. Bread, sugar, and other basic consumer items had disappeared from store shelves. Most people resorted to buying and selling whatever was available in order to supplement their incomes. For those with government jobs, few worked more than 20 hours a week at their regular jobs. Most offices were closed, or stayed open but provided no services. The transportation and the health care systems virtually collapsed. Living conditions were desperate throughout the country. Industrial production almost came to a standstill.

In addition to all these problems, Ghana was also going through a major drought. Crops failed. In March 1983, wildfires swept through the country, destroying the meager, remaining food supplies. Many farmers were devastated. They lost their crops from the previous year and did not have seed for the next year; they had lost their livelihood. To make matters worse, about one million Ghanaians who had been working illegally in Nigeria were deported. Their return swelled the population to a breaking point. They needed food, housing, and jobs. In desperation, the radical Marxist government turned to the International Monetary Fund and World Bank, "imperialist capitalist exploiters," for assistance.

STRUCTURAL ADJUSTMENT AND THE (P)NDC (1983–2000)

In exchange for making major changes in economic policy, Ghana received help from the IMF and the World Bank. Some of the changes were devaluation of the cedi, cutbacks in government expenditure on health and education, and privatization of state-owned industries. For example, in 1983, the American dollar exchanged for 2.75 cedis, but in 1989 it was 650 cedis. Things got a lot worse before they began to get better. The Rawlings government stuck tightly with the harsh medicine. Opposition to the Rawlings regime was crushed viciously. Multiple coup attempts failed. The price of cocoa was increased again and the tax burden on cacao farmers was reduced. Private investment was encouraged again. Ghana became the obedient child of the IMF and World Bank.

Responding to pressure from their new overseers, the Rawlings government introduced a multiparty democracy in

1992 with a new constitution. The PNDC transformed itself into a new party, the National Democratic Congress (NDC). It established the rules for the election and, of course, won. The opposition National Patriotic Party (NPP) claimed that the NDC cheated. In 1996, however, amidst hectic competition from the opposition parties, the NDC won again. The political and economic direction remained unchanged, and the stability began to help. Finally, in 2000, Rawlings's time was up. The constitution permits a president to serve only two terms, so he could not run for president again. The NPP presidential candidate, John Kuffour, defeated Rawlings's former Vice-President, Professor Atta Mills.

GOVERNING GHANA TODAY

The Constitution of the Fourth Republic declares Ghana to be a unitary republic with sovereignty residing in the Ghanaian people. The document reflects lessons learned from the previous constitutions of 1957, 1960, 1969, and 1979, and incorporates ideas drawn from the British and American constitutional models. It divides powers among a president, parliament, cabinet, a Council of State, and an independent judiciary. Government is elected by universal suffrage. One controversial provision of the Constitution, which is sure to be contested, protects members and appointees of the PNDC from liability for any official act or omission during the years of PNDC rule.

Executive authority is established in the Office of the Presidency, together with his Council of State. The president is head of state, head of government, and commander-in-chief of the armed forces. He also appoints the vice-president and cabinet ministers. According to the Constitution, more than half of the ministers of state must be appointed from among members of Parliament. The major political parties include the National Democratic Congress (NDC), led by former president, Jerry John Rawlings, the New Patriotic Party (NPP), led by John Kuffour, the current President, People's National

In January 2001, the leader of the National Patriotic Party, John Kuffour, was inaugurated as Ghana's president after having defeated Jerry Rawlings's Vice-President, Atta Mills, in the election of 2001. Ghana's constitution, based on the American and British models, established the country as a republic with sovereignty residing in the people.

Convention, and People's Convention Party, successor to Kwame Nkrumah's original party

The country is divided into ten administrative regions, 110 districts, 58 town or area councils, 108 zonal councils, and

626 area councils. The local government system consists of a Regional Coordinating Council and a District Assembly Structure. The District Assemblies are either Metropolitan (population over 250,000), Municipal (population over 95,000), or District (population 75,000 and over). There are 3 Metropolitan Assemblies, 4 Municipal Assemblies, and 103 District Assemblies. Seventy percent of the membership of District Assemblies is by election, while the President appoints 30 percent and also the District Chief Executive. The District Assembly is the local arm of the government. It seeks to integrate political, administrative, and developmental support to achieve an equitable distribution of power, wealth, and geographically dispersed development.

The structure and power of the judiciary are independent of the two other branches of government. The Supreme Court has broad powers of judicial review. It is authorized by the Constitution to rule on the constitutionality of any legislation or executive action at the request of any aggrieved citizen. The hierarchy of courts largely follows the British system. The hierarchy, called the Superior Court of Judicature, is composed of the Supreme Court of Ghana, the Court of Appeal, the High Court of Justice, regional tribunals, and such lower courts or tribunals as Parliament may establish. The courts have jurisdiction over all civil and criminal matters.

To conclude, Ghana has had a turbulent and unstable political history. With the 2000 peaceful transition of government to President Kuffour, the storms seem to be over. Political stability has cleared the clouds of economic uncertainty. The economy has been placed on solid footing, suggesting a bright and prosperous future. New investment is pouring into the country. Barring a repeat of the turbulent history, it looks like Ghana, the star of Black Africa, is ready to shine once again.

Handicrafts such as the making of pottery is only one small part of the diverse and rich economy of Ghana.

6

Making a Living in Ghana

Compared to the United States, Ghanaians are very poor. In 2000, Ghana's Gross National Income (GNI) per person, the average income of each Ghanaian for one year, was only US$350. In the United States, the income per person for 2000 was US$34,100. However, compared to other African countries, Ghana's GNI is high. Excluding South Africa, the continent's richest country, the average GNI for Sub-Saharan Africa was only US$299.

Due to better living conditions, Americans also live much longer than Ghanaians. Life expectancy measures the average number of years a child born today will live. In 2000, life expectancy was 77 years in the United States, but only 58 years for Ghana. Because the average in other Sub-Saharan African countries was only 47 years, Ghanaians, by comparison, live much longer. In fact, Ghana has the highest life expectancy among all Sub-Saharan African countries, including South Africa with only 48 years. For most Ghanaians, however, life is hard. This chapter reveals the exciting challenges to livelihood in Ghana. It provides information about jobs, incomes, and daily life.

By African standards, Ghana has a diverse and rich resource base. The country is mainly agricultural. Most of its workers are farmers. Farms are generally small, mostly providing food for the farmer's family. Cacao is the major cash crop. Other farm produce includes corn, rice, sorghum, millet, cassava, yams, peanuts, coffee, coconuts, bananas, and citrus fruit.

Ghana also has established a successful program of non-traditional agricultural products for export, including pineapples, cashews, and pepper. Ghana's pineapples are especially sweet and juicy and are in great demand through-out Europe and the Middle East.

Ghana primarily exports raw materials and imports manufactured goods. The main exports include agricultural products such as cacao beans and products, timber, coffee, copra, cut flowers, fruit, and minerals. The main imports include fuel, machinery, petroleum products, chemical products, consumer goods, and crude oil. Cocoa and gold are the leading sources of foreign exchange.

MINING

Ghana's mineral exports include gold, diamonds, manganese, and bauxite. Petroleum is extracted in small quantities offshore between Saltpond and Cape Coast, and exploration continues for other oil and gas resources. Ghana possesses substantial bauxite reserves. Bauxite is smelted into aluminum. High-quality sand in the Tarkwa mining area provides the basis for a small but important glass industry. Cement factories have been developed at Tema and Takoradi.

Gold is the king of Ghana's minerals. More than 90 percent of the gold production comes from underground mines in the Ashanti, Western, and Central Regions. Ashanti Goldfield Company (AGC), by far the largest and most profitable, is located in Obuasi in the Ashanti Region. Other important gold mining towns include Tarkwa, Prestea, and Bogoso in the Western Region and Dunkwa-Offin in the Central region.

Primarily industrial grade (non-gem) diamonds are extracted from alluvial gravels in the Birim River Basin. More than 11 million carats of proven and probable reserves are located about 70 miles (113 kilometers) northwest of Accra in Akwatia and Kibi in the Eastern Region. The main producer is the state-owned Ghana Consolidated Diamonds (GCD). Before the government established the Precious Minerals Marketing Corporation (PMMC) to purchase minerals from small, frequently illegal, producers, as much as 70 percent of Ghana's diamonds were smuggled out of the country. The PMMC has helped to improve Ghana's production.

Ghana is one of the world's leading exporters of manganese, a metal frequently alloyed with steel for greater strength and hardness. It has reserves exceeding 60 million tons (54.6 million metric tons). With efficient management and stable world market prices, manganese should contribute substantially to the national economy. Manganese is mined mainly in Nsuta in the Western Region.

There are also huge quantities of bauxite. Currently, production is running at about half its potential, and all of the output is exported. This is a major waste in the economy. If bauxite were processed locally, it would provide many jobs, stimulate other industries, and generate much revenue. The main mining areas include Awaso and Bibiani in the Western Region.

The country's mineral deposits have a very interesting geography. Most of the gold, diamond, manganese, and bauxite deposits occur within the southwestern, western, and extreme northern parts of the country. Western and Ashanti regions have the greatest concentration of mining activity. The area within 60 miles (97 kilometers) radius of Dunkwa-Offin in the central Region accounts for about 90 percent of Ghana's mineral export production.

ENERGY PRODUCTS

Ghana struggles with energy production to support industry. The main source of electricity supply is the Volta River Authority (VRA) power plant at Akosombo. Volta Aluminum Company (VALCO) consumes approximately 60 percent of the total electricity produced by the Akosombo dam. Ghana also exports electricity to neighboring Togo and Benin. A second hydroelectric plant is at Kpong, about 25 miles (40 kilometers) downstream from Akosombo. A third dam at Bui on the Black Volta River is being considered, as well as are other sites with potential for power generation on the Pra, Tano, White Volta, and Ankobra rivers. Increasing Ghana's sources of power is important if the country is to avoid the rolling power outages during long periods of drought.

Although commercial quantities of offshore oil reserves were discovered in the 1970s, by 1990 production remained negligible. The Ghana National Petroleum Corporation (GNPC) is charged to explore and produce petroleum products in the country through agreements with a number of foreign firms. One project that may expand Ghana's energy sources is the West African Gas Pipeline, which would transport natural gas to Ghana, Togo, and Benin from Nigeria.

AGRICULTURAL EXPORTS

Ever since colonialism, forestry has always been an important contributor to Ghana's economy. The sector, however, faces several problems. The most important is severe deforestation. A century ago, Ghana's tropical

Running a rural gas station provides this man's living. A Ghanaian typist earns about 500,000 cedis a month (about US$70). That is three times the minimum wage in Ghana and about twice the country's per capita income.

hardwood forest extended from near the middle of the country southward to the sea. Moreover, nearly half the country was covered with forests, which included 680 species of trees including several varieties of mahogany. Most of this wood has been cut. By the early 1990s, only about one-third of the country was still forested, and not all of this was of commercial value. Many factors explain the loss of forests. In addition to extensive logging, they include clearing and burning for agriculture, and cutting for fuel

Cacao pods, from which cocoa and chocolate are derived, are grown primarily by small farmers. Ghana was the world's leading producer of cacao in the 1960s. Farmers are optimistic about improving production, although world prices and the weather bring uncertainty to farming.

wood or making charcoal that people depend upon to cook their meals. Unless some alternative source of energy becomes widely accessible in rural areas, the forests will continue to be under sustained pressure.

Cacao is grown in the forested areas where rainfall is adequate. Peasant farmers grow most of Ghana's cacao on small plots usually less than 10 acres (4 hectares) in size. Although Ghana was the world's largest cacao producer in the early 1960s, by the early 1980s production had dwindled. Aging cacao trees, widespread disease, bad weather, and low producer prices were important contributory factors. The Ghana Cocoa Board manages the earnings from the export of cacao beans. Most of these problems have been addressed, and farmers remain enthusiastic.

Two major problems, however, remain outside their control: weather and global cocoa prices. Because farmers depend solely on rainfall for growing cacao, seasonal variations in rainfall directly affect productivity. Also, the unstable world price makes cacao production a risky business. Because the Ghana government guarantees a fixed price for the cacao crop each season, production should increase.

TOURISM

Tourism is a recent economic activity in Ghana. However, it has become one of the country's primary sources of foreign income, ranking third in 1997. The government has placed great emphasis on further tourism support and development by providing incentives and benefits for investors. Incentives are provided for star-rated hotels, approved tourist villages and beaches, and holiday recreational resorts. Investors are developing other tourist attractions, such as waterfalls, beaches, forts, castles, and historical sites. They are also investing in specialized restaurants, tourist coaches, and buses.

Incentives in this sector include tax exemptions on building properties for three years in addition to investment and depreciation allowances. Revenue from tourism has increased gradually, with most of the tourists coming from Nigeria, the United Kingdom, Côte d'Ivoire, the United States, and Germany. The Ghana Tourist Board and Ghana Tourist Development Company supervise the tourism industry. Star-rated hotels are located at Accra, Tema, Takoradi, and Kumasi, and there is a hotel at Akosombo overlooking Lake Volta.

Some of Ghana's tourist attractions include the slave castles and forts, beautiful beaches, wildlife protected areas, and national game parks. Bui National Park in Mole in the Northern Region has hippos, a variety of antelopes, and many bird species. Boabeng-Fiema monkey sanctuary in Brong-Ahafo Region is a special attraction, as is the crocodile pond in Paga.

The favorite destination for ecotourists is the Kakum National Park. This beautiful park is home to elephants, monkeys, and elusive bongo antelopes that roam among more than 300 rare species of birds, and countless numbers of butterflies, reptiles, and amphibians. Despite its vast natural endowment of plant and animal species, the greatest attraction of Kakum is the wonderful 7-link treetop walkway that allows ecotourists to look down on the tropical rain-forest ecosystem stretching below.

MANUFACTURING AND INDUSTRY

Although Ghana's economy is based mainly on subsistence agriculture, the industrial sector plays an important part by producing goods from local primary products. Ghana's industrial base is relatively advanced compared to that of many other African countries. Industries include textiles, steel (using scrap metal), tires, oil refining, flour milling, beverages, tobacco, simple consumer goods, and automobile assembly. Ghana's major trading partners include Germany, Switzerland, France, the Netherlands, United Kingdom, Japan, and the United States, along with

A fabric stall is crammed from floor to ceiling with colorful fabrics in a Cape Coast, Ghana, shop.

neighboring Nigeria. The country relies on grants from some of these countries to fund areas of development.

SELLERS, SELLERS, SELLERS

If you were in Ghana for one day and you were just an onlooker traveling about in a car or bus, what would you see in the streets? A typical scene at a stoplight might be something like the following. You arrive at a red traffic light. Some traffic grinds to a halt as others begin to move in response to their green light. Horns are blaring. Right-of-way? What does that mean? Go when you can!

There are so many people in the streets, milling around in the traffic—men, women, and children, some of them surprisingly young. Call it a human traffic jam! They are carrying various items on their heads: baskets, boxes, and containers. What is in them? Why are they coming up and knocking on your windows? These are salespeople, business-men and women, and vendors, looking for a chance to sell you something. They hiss loudly to get your attention. When you look in their direction, they enthusiastically display their stuff with wide grins. They sell all kinds of things, some practical, others not. Displayed items include bagged water, food, including bread, hard-boiled eggs, apples, and candy items, as well as tennis rackets, inflatable beach balls, insect repellents, wrist watches, and even puppies.

Why are these people, some of whom are very young, barely ten years old, so zealous and persistent? If you show any interest in the merchandise, they get to work. "How much you pay? I will give you good price!" If you like it, you may bargain through the slightly opened window and make the purchase. Until the deal is clinched, they will pursue you eagerly, following you along the street through the chaotic human and vehicular traffic.

When there are foreigners (usually lighter-skinned or white people) around, all salespeople become terribly charming, especially the children, who specialize in winking and smiling adorably. Sometimes, you just can't say no. Because they know exactly what they are doing, they succeed and you give in. But wait. Why are so many more people suddenly chasing you? It is because you've made a purchase. You have just given yourself away as someone who has money to spend. Now are you expected to buy everything in the street!

This selling in the streets constitutes the livelihood of the

Street peddlers carrying their goods on their heads, small shops, and open markets comprise Ghana's retail trade. Peddlers sell everything from food to tennis balls. Haggling for the best bargain is the way of doing business, and Ghanaian merchants are very aggressive in selling their merchandise

majority of these people. They may depend on that next sale for the evening meal. It is rather sad because not everyone needs two-dozen eggs, or an umbrella, or hat at that particular moment. What happens to the money that is made? Does the seller have a supervisor who collects the money at the end? Where do they get the items that they sell? Why do they always have so much of it, and why is it usually irrelevant to your needs? All this and more contributes to Ghana's informal economy. The government tries to get these children to go to school and stay. Many of them return to their business

A Ghanaian tailor can custom make clothes for next to nothing. Most Ghanaians earn their livings by traditional means. Farming and mining are important, but tourism and manufacturing are growing in importance. Although Ghana is a poor country by American standards, its income per person is high for Africa.

as soon as school is out. The little money they earn on each sale is desperately needed at home.

NATIONAL ECONOMIC POLICY

Ghana has pursued stringent economic reforms since 1983 under the guidance of the World Bank and the International Monetary Fund. The economic recovery program includes increasing privatization of government-owned industries.

Heavily dependent on cocoa, gold, and timber exports, economic growth so far has not spread substantially to other areas of the economy. Ghana has a mixed economy, with both government and privately owned industries. This is changing with the program of privatization of state-owned enterprises. Despite an energy crisis in 1998 due to drought, Ghana has managed to continue its economic program and plans to privatize the energy sector.

Although Ghana faced food shortages in the past, they were significantly reduced by the late 1990s. The economy faces a number of challenges; principal among these are the country's high population growth and high illiteracy rates.

A policy of industrialization has resulted in the establishment of a wide range of manufacturing industries producing food products, beverages, tobacco, textiles, clothes, footwear, timber and wood products, chemicals and pharmaceuticals, and metals, including steel and steel products.

Today, Ghana's economy remains dependent on rural agriculture and export of raw materials. Cacao, timber, pineapples, and mining (mainly gold) are the major sources of foreign exchange. The emerging industrial sector's products include cassava, fruits, and cocoa by-products. Beginning in the latter half of 1999, Ghana suffered major economic shock resulting from falling prices for the two main exports, gold and cocoa, and rising prices for petroleum imports. The exchange rate depreciated rapidly in the latter part of 1999, and inflation increased significantly. As the terms of trade worsened, the exchange rate depreciation and rising inflation continued through 2000. Timely government intervention in early 2000 tightened monetary policy, postponed public expenditures, and raised taxes. These actions have produced some economic stability and reduced inflation.

The political situation has also stabilized. On January 7, 2001, a new government headed by President John A.

Kuffour, took office in what constituted the first democratic transfer of power in 19 years. Kuffour's New Patriotic Party (NPP) won the presidential vote and parliamentary majority against the former ruling party, the National Democratic Congress (NDC), led by Rawlings. The peaceful political transition is widely regarded as a major achievement for Ghana and for the region. In response to the continued economic and structural reforms supported by the IMF and the World Bank, and the political stability, Ghana's economy is beginning to rebound.

Currently, Ghana is about as poor as it can be simply because of all the debts it has accumulated through the years. All the new projects that previous leaders tried to initiate cost money that Ghana didn't have. Unfortunately, many of these projects were not completed before the initiating governments were removed from power. Most of the projects were abandoned as soon as the leader was removed. Now, it is payback time and the obvious options, widespread depression or defaulting on international loans, are not attractive.

This is what Ghana chose to do. It adopted the Heavily Indebted Poor Country (HIPC) program in April 2001. This is an international program for reducing the debt of the world's poorest and most heavily indebted countries. In addition to coming out and telling everyone that they are broke, HIPC countries must implement some economic reforms and reduce poverty. In exchange, the countries to which debts are owed write off or cancel the debts. This enables Ghana to start work on repairing the country from the ground up. If the country had chosen not to declare to the world that they had gone HIPC, it would still be struggling with the enormous debts and no possibility of repaying them.

The economy, once advertised as an IMF/World Bank showpiece, has suffered badly as a result of low commodity prices for cocoa and gold. Today, however, it is beginning to improve. Thanks to HIPC, debt service payments have reduced significantly. This has released money for important poverty relief projects. Among the unemployed and the poor, expectations for the new government are very high. Unfortunately, development may be slow. Ghana does, however, now have the basic elements in place, which is essential to economic recovery and future growth.

Life is not easy in Ghana. Most Ghanaians spend half of their monthly incomes on food alone. Although Ghanaians have a warm, friendly attitude, economic hardship is common and jobs are scarce.

7

Life in Ghana Today

L iving in Ghana today is not always easy. Jobs are scarce and
for those who have jobs salaries are meager. In May 2002,
the minimum wage for a full day's work was less than $1.
How is one going to eat, assuming they don't have a steady or
well-paying job? Food is very expensive. Most people spend at
least 50 percent of their monthly income on food alone. Where
is a person's next meal coming from? What if one gets sick?
Good quality health care is not readily available, except for those
who can pay the high prices private hospitals demand. Despite
all these difficulties, Ghanaians have a wonderful, loving, warm
attitude, and are always smiling. The economy is headed in the
right direction, and the future looks quite bright. In this chapter,
some of the things that affect Ghana and its people today will
be considered.

In 2000, of every thousand children born, 66 died before their first birthday (compared to 7 per 1,000 in the United States). Malnutrition among children under five years old was 25 percent, while the number of children who died before their fifth birthday per 1,000 live births was a high 112.1. Over 75 percent of urban residents live within 30 minutes of a health facility, compared to only 30 percent of people living in rural areas. In fact, in Upper East and Upper West, only 15 percent of the population lives within 30 minutes of a health facility.

In 2002, about 3 percent of the adult population (ages 15 to 49) was estimated to be HIV positive. Ghana's HIV-AIDS problem is much smaller than in most other African countries. For example, Côte d'Ivoire, the original source of Ghana's HIV-AIDS cases, has an adult rate of about 11%. There are almost twice as many female AIDS patients as males with the disease in Ghana, and rural areas tend to have more cases than urban areas.

Malaria is the most commonly reported disease and the leading cause of death among children under five years old. It is also a major cause of sickness among adults. In fact, most people suffer malarial symptoms three or four times a year. Anemia and malnutrition also are widespread. Cholera is always present in some areas due to persistent poverty and poor sanitation. In 1998, stroke, hypertension, and diabetes were leading causes of adult death.

What is life like in Ghana today? Suppose someone is sick with malaria. What happens? That depends on whether he is rich or poor and where he lives. Among the treatment options is a new term—"cash-and-carry."

The cash-and-carry system is a product of the structural adjustment program which the IMF and the World Bank prescribed and which Ghana has faithfully implemented since 1983. It involves the removal of government subsidies on health care. This means health care costs more. Since its introduction, cash-and-carry appears to have taken health services away from the people. Many do not favor the system because it severely limits the treatment options of the poor.

A 2001 article in the *New Internationalist Magazine* reported one physician as saying, "The system is stinking and dehumanizing. Patients who do not have the ability to pay for medical services are turned away from hospitals only to die at home. The poor, the disabled and accident victims are being asked to pay on the spot before getting medical attention. This system has no human face. Our health service is in confusion."

In fact, health care has reached a point where many Ghanaians go to a pharmacist instead of a doctor to avoid paying consultation fees. Many people do not have money to pay for something as simple as a painkiller. The situation is quite serious, and many pharmacists have given out drugs without charge because of the circumstances.

Some people try to get health care without paying for it. For example, at the Komfo Anokye Teaching Hospital in Kumasi, as many as two in five patients reportedly escape from the hospital without payment. To prevent this, each new patient is now required to pay 100,000 cedis (about $15, an astronomical amount since the minimum daily wage is less than one dollar) to the hospital on admission.

The quality of health care also varies depending on whether it is provided by a government or private health facility. Private health facilities, with fees beyond what most Ghanaians can afford, provide excellent health care. In government health facilities, the quality of care is deteriorating very fast because of government cutbacks. Parts of the Korle-Bu Teaching Hospital in Accra, the largest hospital in Ghana, have been reduced to a center of human neglect and administrative lapses. Mosquitoes are present and, sometimes, mice run rampant in the wards. A visitor to Korle-Bu recently said, "This place is no longer a life-saving environment, but a death trap. You will certainly contract a disease if you come here."

A final example of the humiliation medical patients endure is offered by Betty Krampa, a prisoner at the hospital. She had just given birth and was sitting on her rickety metal bed in the corridor of Tarkwa General Hospital. She was not allowed to leave until she paid. This is called cash-and-carry. Patients pay for everything—surgery, drugs, blood, and even the cotton wool. Betty's parents are dead. Her husband is out of work. Her jailers are as ashamed as she is. User fees, however, have to be collected to keep the hospital going.

The government is working hard to replace the dehumanizing cash-and-carry system with a national health insurance plan. In 2002, forty-two districts had health insurance programs in place. All 110 districts expect to have plans by 2004.

EMIGRATION OF SKILLED WORKERS

The country also suffers from many experienced health workers leaving their jobs. In fact, most are leaving the country. Due to the difficult economic circumstances, they are leaving to find better-paying positions in Europe, the United States, South Africa, or elsewhere. Unless something is done very quickly, Ghana faces a serious crisis in health personnel. Unfortunately, the government cannot match the attractive salary packages offered by recruiting agencies from developed countries such as the UK. The Ministry of Health reports that about 662 health personnel, comprising 60 doctors, 363 nurses, and 239 pharmacists, left the country to seek better conditions abroad in 2001 alone.

Health workers are not the only ones leaving Ghana. In the 1990s, an estimated 10 to 20 percent of all Ghanaians were living abroad. Based on the current population, that is two to four million people. Deteriorating standards of living and spreading poverty resulting from economic reforms and structural adjustment programs are the primary reasons for emigration (out migration). To obtain a better livelihood for themselves and their families, skilled Ghanaians have simply left the country. This has produced great losses of highly skilled professionals. The emigration pattern is quite mixed, but the United States, Germany, Italy, and Nigeria are the top four preferred destinations.

Remittances from Ghanaians living outside Ghana contribute an ever-increasing share of Ghana's foreign exchange earnings. In fact, they are becoming a major factor in Ghana's economic recovery. In 2000, official money transfers from Ghana's international migrants exceeded $400 million, and it was the third largest foreign exchange earner, after gold and cocoa. In fact, one source put the estimated total remittances figure for 2000 at more than one billion dollars. Surely, this is good for Ghana, but who will fill the vacant posts?

INTERNET AND COMPUTER USE

Another important issue today in Ghana is computer and Internet use. In 2000, Accra did not have a single Internet cafe. Now the city boasts hundreds of them. Low prices for PCs and new ways of circumventing the phone system to reach Web servers is the major reason. Moreover, many people need to contact their relatives who have left Ghana to seek better living conditions overseas. One hour online costs anywhere from $0.75 to $1.25. This is still very costly in a country where many people earn only that much in a day.

Throughout the country, there are hundreds of Internet service providers. More than 1.3 million people dial up subscribers from plentiful Internet cafes. Accra, the capital of Ghana, is also the high-tech center of West Africa. In Accra, more than 600 shiny new Internet cafes with names like

The Internet has brought important, new employment to Ghana. Companies in the United States send digitized forms to offices in Accra, Ghana's capital, for processing and subsequent data transmission back to the United States.

"Cyberia" and "Mega Internet" compete for business. Most of these cafes are in use night and day by Ghanaians eager to pay for agonizingly slow Internet access to the outside world. In Accra, especially, dilapidated booths have been converted into computer training centers.

In fact, the Internet is emerging as an important employment opportunity with global connections. In a third floor office in the high-rise known as the Pyramid in Accra, hundreds of men and women type at computer keyboards. They are reading American health insurance claims on their computer screens. Each claim form has been digitized in the

United States by Aetna, the large insurer, and sent over a computer network to Accra. Here a typist pulls the name, address, and other personal information from the form, entering it into a new electronic form that is then sent back to the United States.

In a similar move, New York City traffic tickets are being processed in an Internet center in Accra. Just days after the tickets are written out on New York City streets, they are scanned and sent as digital photographs to computers in a small office in downtown Accra. There, workers try to make out the unfamiliar street names (Dyckman, Flatbush, Hudson) while transcribing the handwritten scrawl of New York City police officers into searchable databases. They type the offender's name, address, fine, and offense location into a searchable database that is sent back to New York. It can then be stored electronically and used to generate payment notices. It is good work, by Ghanaian standards. The typists earn 500,000 cedis a month (almost $70). This is three times the Ghanaian minimum wage and more than twice the average per capita income.

SKIN BLEACHING AND THE REJECTION OF BLACKNESS

Some Ghanaians are locked in a practice of skin bleaching or attempting to lighten the skin. Ghanaian officials have also been trying unsuccessfully to ban bleaching products. Public service broadcasting campaigns warn about the harmful side effects of skin bleaching, including skin disease and skin cancer. Hydroquinone, the leading ingredient in most skin lighteners, operates by hindering the making of melanin (the single chemical responsible for coloring the skin pigments in human beings), causing dark colors to fade as bleached cells replace older cells.

The desire for lighter skin has been difficult to discourage. During colonialism, it was stylish to wear European clothing and talk like a European. It was also important to look and feel like a European. In salons, the advertisements almost always depict a very light-skinned girl with straight hair. In fact, some women do not feel attractive unless they are light-skinned. Oddly, in Ghana and other parts of Africa, some dark-skinned people want to be lighter, but in the United States, most light-skinned people want to be darker. This is why tanning booths and sun worshipping are widespread. However, tanning also can cause skin disease and cancer. Yet in Ghana, it appears that the lighter one is, the more attractive and financially stable he/she must be. Even those who live in villages bleach their skin, because they think that by doing so they are seen as somebody who is important or well-to-do.

Many people who bleach don't find help until it is too late. Despite the service announcements and "Stop Bleaching" campaigns on TV and the radio, people do not listen. Some end up with such serious skin disease that they cannot safely go out into the sun. When this happens, they turn to something new. They use creams from local markets in an attempt to turn their skin back to its original complexion.

Physicians say that bleaching for more than two years causes irreparable damage. Doctors now see cases where they cannot apply stitches because the skin has weakened to the point where it falls apart. Surgical complications, such as difficulty in suturing the skin and poor healing of surgical wounds, result from bleaching.

MONEY, RESPECT, AND THE ELDERLY

In most parts of Ghana, money equals respect. The elderly are respected by all simply because of their age. One young man remarks, "We think that the old have a certain blessing, merely because of their age. When you respect and honor them, they will bless you, and that blessing will be forever on your life. In this same way, when they curse you it will be forever." In general, Ghanaians believe that with aging

This 107-year-old woman is the exception to the rule. Life expectancy in Ghana is about 57 years (compared to 80 years for the United States). Life expectancy in Ghana in 1957 was 44 years. Today, Ghana has one of the highest life expectancies in Africa.

comes knowledge and wisdom that can be conveyed to the younger generations. Thus, the elderly are entitled to be respected, in particular by those who are younger.

This kind of respect is the basis of the care that elderly people enjoy from their children or other relatives. Nonetheless, many older people today complain that the young lack respect. Old age in itself no longer encourages respect. Both young and old point out that respect is bestowed primarily upon those who turned their life into a success. A great way of showing respect is with money, which is a natural topic of conversation for the elderly. Most often, the discussion centers on money and what money can buy or has bought. In Ghana today, the most convincing proof of a successful life is money. The more money you have, the more respect you will gain. Giving money is a way of showing respect. Traditions that used to be maintained by offerings and gift giving—marriage, birth, funeral celebrations, or apprenticeship for example—are now linked with the exchange of money. Complaints about money are common methods for lamenting the current era.

It has become more and more difficult to survive without money. In the past, people could support themselves fairly well even if they had little or no money. They could bring produce from the farm, which met most of their needs. Now, most food has to be bought. The need for money makes the younger generation leave home to find favorable employment in a larger town or in the cities. This leaves the elderly without care and respect. Even though money and respect are linked together and one usually equals the other, the elderly are always put first and are treated with the utmost admiration and held in highest regard.

ONE DAY IN ACCRA, GHANA

Just imagine. We have one day to spend in Accra, Ghana, the geographic center of the world. What will it be like? That depends on what day it is. How about Sunday? You wake up about 7:00 A.M. and get something to eat. Breakfast probably includes a cup of tea, with milk and sugar, and sweet bread with margarine. After breakfast you go in the bathroom to take a shower and get ready for church service. Almost everyone goes to church on Sunday.

You undress, go into the shower and turn it on. No water. You get out, cover yourself, and walk to the kitchen to get a bucket of water. If you have lived in Ghana all your life, you know how to scoop the water on to your body with a cupped hand. If you can't do that, you need a cup. Lather yourself, scoop water from the bucket with the cup, and pour it over

Downtown Accra, where street vendors selling wares off their heads walk by the foreign exchange bureau.

yourself. The shower is still refreshing, even if a little strange. After you dress (church service in Ghana is a dress-up affair) you go to stand by the roadside to get a taxi to go to church.

It is a beautiful day. The temperature is about 75°F (24° C) and the humidity is about 80 percent. Many other people are waiting for taxis too, so you have a lot of competition. Three taxis pass by, and they do not stop because they are full. Finally one taxi stops, and everybody rushes. But there is room for only one person. Finally, after some skillful positional strategizing, and 45 minutes later, you get to church. You are only 10 minutes late, which is not bad at all. Sometimes, you are one hour late.

The church is packed. The music is wonderful. Most people are dancing. The voices of the congregation fill the building. This is awesome. Then there is the preaching. In a thunderous booming voice, the Pastor announces, "Jesus came to take away your sickness; your sorrow; your shame. Cheer up, you have victory in Jesus; over sickness; over disease; over poverty." "Amen! Amen! Amen!" you shout with the others, getting louder each time. After 45 minutes of encouraging preaching you are ready for another week. Time to go get some lunch. You decide to go Paloma Restaurant. Getting a taxi is a bit easier this time.

Paloma is a very nice, American-style restaurant. You can even see it on the web (*http://www.africaonline.com.gh/Paloma/fastfood.html*). The smartly dressed waitress flashes the warm welcoming Ghanaian smile as she leads you to a table. You decide on fufu and peanut butter soup. Yum! Your full meal costs just about one dollar. Not bad, but that is about how much most people earn in one day.

You take a taxi to the Accra Sport Stadium to see a soccer game. The game starts at 4:00 P.M. Who is playing today? It could be the Ghana Black Stars, the national soccer team, against Nigeria Green Eagles. Or it could be the two national giants, Accra Hearts of Oak and Kumasi Asante Kotoko. The stadium is packed to capacity. The crowd is loud. The environment is electric. With faces and bodies painted, the fans are drumming, dancing, and having a good time. After 90 minutes of the best soccer, it is time to go home. Getting a taxi is tricky, but you finally get home about 8:00 P.M., ninety minutes after the game ended.

You are thinking about the special treat in the fridge, the juicy pineapple. As you approach your house, you notice that the electricity is out. There are no lights. It is dark. You anticipated this. So you turn on your flashlight and make your way home. First, you get the hurricane lamp and light it.

Then you go to the refrigerator and get your treasure. You take it to the table and enjoy it. It is delicious, even if a little warm. A wonderful day. Time to go to bed. There is no need to turn out the lights. They are already out. Good night!

Uniformed school children visiting the Aburi Botanical Gardens smile and enjoy having their pictures taken, which is very typical of Ghanaian youth. Ghanaian families place a high priority on raising children in a happy, nurturing environment, which is why so many Ghanaian children are seen smiling.

8

What is the Black Star's Future?

G hana has seen the good, the bad, and the ugly throughout its history. The country has survived slavery, numerous military takeovers, and grinding poverty and still come through with smiles on its people's faces. What is in store for the future? As seen in the previous chapters, Ghana is blessed with beautiful, hardworking people, an inviting climate, and an excellent geographic location. The natural landscape is suitable for producing many crops, including cacao and pineapples. It also provides ample natural resources, including much gold. Nature has endowed Ghana with abundant potential for greatness. The question is, how will that greatness be achieved? With some hard work on the economy and a steady government to rely on, Ghana could flourish.

One of the issues the country needs to seriously address is agriculture. Irrigation systems are still quite unpopular with

Ghanaian people. In spite of the considerable progress made within the agricultural sector in recent years, Ghana's agriculture continues to operate at very low levels of efficiency. With the right approaches, Ghana can feed itself and many of its neighbors with food to spare.

Ghana has made steady educational progress over recent decades, nearly doubling adult literacy rates from 1970 to 2000. The government's goal is to increase access to education for all divisions of society. Another dimension of increasing the quality of education is providing Internet access in classrooms. The "Bridges to the Future Initiative" (BFI) seeks to improve the basic skills, literacy, and entry-level vocational skills for out-of-school youth and young adults in poor communities. The BFI will focus principally on assisting youth and primary school dropouts who seek to reenter the regular cycle of schooling. It will also help many others who have never attended school and those in alternative schools or young adults continuing in occupational education programs. BFI seeks to do this using the Internet.

A popular assumption of the BFI-Ghana approach is that the "digital divide" is not purely one of access to hardware. Rather, it is a divide of education and skills separating the rich and poor. As a result, literacy and high-tech competence need to be addressed at the same time with information and instructional resources that can be delivered in a culturally appropriate manner. It must be done at a lower cost and higher quality than has been possible before. Many such efforts are currently underway, targeted at the young businessmen on the streets of Ghana's large cities.

WORLD NEIGHBORS

In Samwo, northern Ghana, drought comes often and destroys the annual harvest and withers people's hopes of storing any grain for the coming year. This causes serious concern for those who need to feed their families if rain doesn't come. For this reason, saving for sunny days is a tradition for families in the dry savannah region of West Africa. If the harvest is good, families keep enough sorghum and millet to last two years. They fatten some goats and chickens and perhaps a cow if they are lucky. Animals are comparable to "walking savings accounts" that provide protein or cash in a time of need.

The problem is that drought has become more and more common. Once the grain is used up and the families' animals have been eaten or sold, there is no safety net to fall back on. Some families may be forced to eat their seeds, sell their tools, or even worse, give up their land. Many will cut down trees to make charcoal for sale in the market. Harvesting trees, however, increases the risk of drought, fueling a cycle of poverty and environmental degradation.

Credit is available from local moneylenders, but they demand interest rates of 100 percent or more. However, the people in Samwo are feeling more optimistic about their future. With help from World Neighbors, a UMCOR partner, they formed a self-help group that serves as a credit union, making small loans at reasonable interest rates. The group sets its own interest rates, in this case at 20 percent. Each member uses the loans as they choose. This group is only one of hundreds of self-help organizations that have sprung into action with World Neighbors support. With just a little help and an addition to savings, people are able to make it through hard times.

SO LONG, FAREWELL

So what do you think? Is Ghana a great country? Let's recap all that you have learned so far about Ghana through this book. First, Ghana used to be called the Gold Coast because of all the gold on the coast! Second, it has some beautiful landscape and some boring landscape, but the rain forests and jungles are definitely the best. Third, the temperature is favorable and never goes below 50°F (10°C) or above 100°F (38°C). Fourth, Volta Lake, the world's largest man-made reservoir, is in Ghana. Fifth, Ghana was the first Black African country to gain its independence from colonial rule. Sixth, Ghana was the major source for slave shipments to the Americas. Seventh, Ghanaian people are extremely friendly and warm and welcoming. Eighth, there are many ethnic groups and languages in Ghana. Ninth, in Ghana, God is very important. Tenth, Ghanaians are very creative and resourceful in selling, selling, selling. Eleventh, kente and adinkra are native to Ghana and are very colorful and attractive cloths and prints. Twelfth, Ghanaian music is incredible; the drumming can be used not only for music, but also for communication. Thirteenth, Ghanaians like to party and have a lot of fun. Fourteenth, food from Ghana is different and delicious. Fifteenth, Ghana has one of the most stable democracies in Africa today. Sixteenth, the economy can use a lot of help, but is getting much better. Seventeenth, cash-and-carry, as related to medical care, needs to be reconsidered. Eighteenth, computer and Internet access are spreading rapidly. Nineteenth, skin bleaching is a big issue on which people are now beginning to take a stand. Twentieth, the elderly are respected by young and old. Twenty-first, giving money is a great way to show respect. Twenty-second, agriculture and farming methods need improvement. Twenty-third, new initiatives such as BFI and World Neighbors are helping to ease the suffering. Twenty-fourth, Ghanaians love to smile. And twenty-fifth, GHANA ROCKS!!!

IT COULD HAPPEN!

If you ever get a chance to travel to West Africa, GO! Do not pass up a chance to visit the geographic center of the world. Go to Ghana and take this book with you. It may take awhile to get used to the humidity and the time difference, but it is all worth it. When you're ready, look around. Tour the national forests and the villages. Try to eat something different, like fufu, or peanut butter soup. Enjoy the delicious pineapples. Enjoy a soccer game. Observe the fancy footwork. You may even pick up a few moves to polish your game! Learn a few words in Twi. People will be happy to teach you. Go to the schools. You won't

Soccer is very popular in Ghana whether played by the national team, the Ghana Black Stars, Accra's team, the Accra Hearts of Oak, or just a local team. Soccer games are exciting events, and when played in Accra's stadium, drumming, dancing, and loud cheering are part of the enjoyment.

believe how happy the kids will be to see you. Have a pen and paper ready. They will want your address. Take a shopping trip to the market. Be ready to sweat. Never in your life will you have another experience like shopping in Ghana!

Get some clothes custom-made. You can afford it; the labor and materials are cheap. Buy some carvings. They make great decorations. Take lots of pictures; be sure your camera has a flash (It is extremely popular with the kids, and they love posing). Take a video camera and get the kids and yourself on tape! Go with a group—the more new people, the better. Listen to Ghanaian music as you travel. Get some chocolate. It is made right in Ghana! Check out the clubs some time. There is cool music and fun people. Buy a new shirt or a dress in the traditional kente design. They're beautiful, comfortable, and wonderful conversation starters. Go to a drumming show. WOW! While you're there, do me a favor: tell them Esther sent you!

Facts at a Glance

Country Name	Republic of Ghana Conventional: Ghana
Location	Central part of West Africa, bordering the Gulf of Guinea, between Côte d'Ivoire to the west, Togo to the east and Burkina Faso to the north.
Area	92,090 square miles (238,513 square kilometers)
Capital	Accra
Climate	Tropical; warm and comparatively dry along southeast coast; hot and humid in southwest; hot and dry in the north.
Terrain	Mostly low plains with dissected plateau in south-central area
Elevation Extremes	Lowest point: sea level at Atlantic Ocean; highest point, Mount Afadjato 2,905 feet (885 meters)
Natural Hazards	Dry, dusty, harmattan winds occur from January to March; droughts
Land Use	Arable land: 12% Permanent Crops: 7% Permanent Pastures: 22% Forests and Woodland: 35% Other:` 24% (1993 est.)
Environmental Issues	Recent drought in north severely affecting agricultural activities; deforestation; overgrazing; soil erosion; poaching and habitat destruction threatens wildlife populations; water pollution; inadequate supplies of potable water
Population	19,894,014
Population Growth Rate	0.79% (2001 estimate; declining)
Life Expectancy	Total Population: 57.24 years Male: 55.86 years Female: 58.66 years (2001 est.)
Nationality	Ghanaian(s)
Ethnic Groups	Black African 99.8% (major tribes: Akan 44%, Moshi-Dagomba 16%, Ewe 13%, Ga 8%), European and other 0.2%

Religions	Indigenous beliefs 9%, Muslim 16%, Christian 69%, Other 6%
Languages	English (official). African languages include Akan, Moshi-Dagomba, Ewe, and Ga
Literacy	64.5%
Type of Government	Constitutional democracy
Head of State	President
Independence	March 6, 1957 (from the United Kingdom)
Administrative Divisions	10 regions: Ashanti, Brong-Ahafo, Central, Eastern, Greater Accra, Northern, Upper East, Upper West, Volta, Western
Flag Description	Three equal horizontal bands of red (top), yellow, and green with a large black five-pointed star centered in the yellow band.
Currency	Ghana cedi (GHC)
Gross Domestic Product	Purchasing power parity—$37.4 billion (2000 est.)
Labor Force by Occupation	Agriculture 60%, Industry 15%, Service 25%
Industries	Mining, lumbering, light manufacturing, aluminum smelting, food processing
Exports	$1.6 billion (2000 estimate). Gold, cocoa, timber, tuna, bauxite, aluminum, manganese ore, diamonds
Imports	$2.2 billion (2000 estimate). Capital equipment, petroleum, foodstuffs.
Transportation	Highways: 24,630 miles (39,640 kilometers) Paved 7,283 miles (11,721 kilometers), including 19 miles (30 kilometers) of expressways Railways: 596 miles (959 kilometers) Airports: 12 (6 with paved runways)

History at a Glance

About 40,000	Early traces of humans in West Africa.
About 4,000 B.C.	Earliest evidence of humans in Gold Coast.
1700 – 1500 B.C.	Kintampo Culture thrives.
1471 A.D.	First Europeans (Portuguese) arrived in Gold Coast.
1482	Elmina Caste built.
1553	First British trading mission arrived.
1562	British begin slave trade in Africa.
1598	Dutch arrived in Cape Coast.
1700	Beginning of Asante Empire under King Osei Tutu.
1750	Slave trade overtakes gold trade in importance.
1820–1902	Series of British and Asante wars:
1823–1824	In Battle of Nsamankow, Asante defeat British Governor Sir Charles MacCarthy and his Fante and Denkyira allies. MacCarthy is killed.
1826	British defeat Asantes in the Battle of Kantamanto near Dodowa.
1831	Governor George Maclean signed treaty with the Asantes.
1863	Asante defeat Britain in Battle of Bobikuma.
1873–1877	Asante King, Kofi Karikari, invaded southern and coastal areas. Major General Sir Garnet Woseley with British expedition forces defeated the Asantes. In Treaty of Fomena 1874, Asante forced to recognize the Independence of all states south of the Pra River.
1888	Nana Agyeman Prempeh I became King of Asante.
1896	British troops marched to Kumasi, led by Sir Francis Scott. Asante King exiled first to the Elmina Castle, then to Sierra Leone, and later to Seychelles.
1900	Arnold Hodgson went to ask for the golden stool, infuriating the Asantes. Yaa Asantewaa, queen mother of Ejisu, leads attack on the British Fort in Kumasi.

1924	Nana Agyemang Prempeh I returned. Died in 1931.
1844	Commander Hill and the Bond of 1844. Coastal states become British protectorate.
1874	Gold mine in Wassa and Asante. Between 1946-1950 gold export rose from 6 million pounds to 9 million pounds.
1878	Tetteh Quarshie brought cocoa from Fernado Po.
1885	Cocoa first exported to Britain.
1897	Aborigines Rights Protection Society.
1898–1927	Railway expansion in Ghana.
1925	Guggisburg Constitution. Legislative Council comprising 15 colonial government officials, 14 non-officials (9 Ghanaians, 6 elected by chiefs and 3 from Accra, Cape Coast and Sekondi). Central Administration was made of the Governor, the Executive Council, and the Legislative Council, which served only in advisory capacity.
1928	Takoradi Harbor built.
1945	United Gold Coast Conversion (UGCC) formed. Kwame Nkrumah as General Secretary. Other officers George Grant (Paa Grant), Akuffo Addo, William Ofori Atta, Obetsebi Lamptey, Ako Agyei, and J Tsiboe. Their aim was Independence for Ghana.
1947	Cocoa Marketing Board (CMB) established.
1947–1951	Political Movements and Nationalism in Ghana.
1948	Riots in the Gold Coast. Nii Kwabena Bone II, an Accra chief, organized the boycott of European and Syrian, Lebanese goods. Ex-servicemen marched on Christianborg Castle to hand petition to the governor about their poor conditions. Repression of demonstration led to 3 dead. UGCC was held responsible and its officers were detained.
1951	Revenue from cocoa was 60 million pounds sterling.
1949	Internal trouble in UGCC. Nkrumah broke off to form his own Convention Peoples' Party (CPP), with the slogan of "Self-Government Now."

1951 First General election. CPP won 34 seats, UGCC 3. Kwame Nkrumah, in prison for positive action, won the seat in central Accra and was released to become the leader of Government business and Prime Minister on March 21, 1952.

1954 New Constitution with assembly and speaker. 104 elected representatives. CPP - 72 seats, Northern People's Party (NPP) - 15, Independents - 11, and Others - 6.

1954 The National Liberation Movement (NLM) formed by linguist Baffour Akoto. Leader was J. B. Danquah, and Dr. K. A. Busia, member. This group wanted a federal government.

1956 Another general election. CPP won 72 of the 104 seats. The NLM and its allies won the remaining seats and so became the parliamentary opposition.

1956 Former British Mandated Togoland voted to join the Gold Coast-Ghana.

1957 Independence, Kwame Nkrumah of CPP is elected Prime Minister.

1960 Ghana declared a republic. One-party presidential system.

1966 Military overthrow of first republic

1969 Second republic, Busia of Progress Party is Prime Minister.

1972 Military overthrow of second republic. General Acheampong as head of state.

1978 Palace coup to restructure military government. General Akuffo as Head of State.

1979 Armed Forces Revolutionary Council military takeover and "housecleaning" exercise. Eight senior military officers, including two former heads of state, were executed.

1979 Third republic. Dr. Hilla Limann of PNP is President.

1981 Overthrow of the PNP government by the PNDC led by Rawlings.

1983 Attempted overthrow of the PNDC by other junior army men. Ghana adopts IMF/World Bank initiated Economic Recovery Program.

1992	Jerry Rawlings of NDC is elected as President.
1996	Jerry Rawlings of NDC is reelected.
2001	John Kuffour (NPP) is elected President.

Further Reading

Berry, LaVerle. *Ghana : A Country Study.* Area Handbook Series, Library of Congress. Washington, DC: U. S. Government Printing Office, 1995.

Blauer, Ettagle and Jason Laure. *Ghana.* Scholastic Library Publishing, September 1999

Briggs, Philip. *Ghana, the Bradt Travel Guide.* 2nd edition, Bradt Publications, September 2001.

Davis, Lucille. *Ghana.* Capstone Press, December 1998.

Hintz, Martin. *Ghana.* Scholastic Library Publishing, April 1987

Levy, Patricia M and P. Levy. *Ghana.* Marshall Cavendish Inc., January 1999.

Some Helpful Websites

Republic of Ghana - Gold Coast of Africa.
http://www.ghana.com/republic/

Central Intelligence Agency. CIA—The World Factbook, Ghana.
www.cia.gov/cia/publications/factbook/geos/gh.html (current).

The Library of Congress Country Studies: Ghana.
http://memory.loc.gov/frd/cs/ghtoc.html

The Ghana Homepage.
http://www.ghanaweb.com/

Index

Index

About the Author

JOSEPH R. OPPONG is Associate Professor of Geography at the University of North Texas in Denton, Texas, and a native of Ghana. He has about 15 years university teaching experience in Ghana, Canada, and the United States. Joseph has served as Chair of the Africa Specialty Group of the Association of American Geographers and as Director of the Medical Geography Specialty Group. His research focuses on medical geography: the geography of disease and health care. Joseph enjoys teaching, research, photography, and his four children, including Esther, the oldest and co-author of this book.

ESTHER D. OPPONG is an active junior in high school. Her hobbies include talking to and meeting people, writing, singing, and playing her guitar. She has been to Ghana once and is eager to go again. This is her first book and she dreams of writing many more.

CHARLES F. ("FRITZ") GRITZNER is Distinguished Professor of Geography at South Dakota University in Brookings. He is now in his fifth decade of college teaching and research. During his career, he has taught more than 60 different courses, spanning the fields of physical, cultural, and regional geography. In addition to his teaching, he enjoys writing, working with teachers, and sharing his love for geography with students. As consulting editor for the MODERN WORLD NATIONS series, he has a wonderful opportunity to combine each of these "hobbies." Fritz has served as both president and executive director of the National Council for Geographic Education and has received the Council's highest honor, the George J. Miller Award for Distinguished Service.